I0483788

Summary

In 2008, Canadian pipeline company TransCanada filed an application with the U.S. Department of State to build the Keystone XL pipeline, which would transport crude oil from the oil sands region of Alberta, Canada, to refineries on the U.S. Gulf Coast. Keystone XL would ultimately have the capacity to transport 830,000 barrels per day, delivering crude oil to the market hub at Cushing, OK, and further to points in Texas. TransCanada plans to build a pipeline spur so that oil from the Bakken formation in Montana and North Dakota can also be carried on Keystone XL.

As a facility connecting the United States with a foreign country, the pipeline requires a Presidential Permit from the State Department. In evaluating such a permit application, the department must determine whether it is in the "national interest," considering the project's potential effects on the environment, economy, energy security, foreign policy, and other factors. Environmental impacts are considered pursuant to the National Environmental Policy Act, and documented by the State Department in an Environmental Impact Statement (EIS). The final EIS was released for the Keystone XL pipeline permit application in August 2011, after which a 90-day public review period began to make the national interest determination. During that time the State Department determined that more information was needed to consider an alternative pipeline route avoiding the environmentally sensitive Sand Hills region of Nebraska, an extensive sand dune formation with highly porous soil and a shallow depth to groundwater recharging the Ogallala aquifer.

The Temporary Payroll Tax Cut Continuation Act of 2011 (P.L. 112-78) required the Secretary of State to approve or deny the project within 60 days. On January 18, 2012, the State Department, with the President's consent, denied the Keystone XL permit, citing insufficient time under this deadline to properly assess the reconfigured project. Subsequently, TransCanada announced that it would proceed with development of the pipeline segment connecting Cushing, OK, to the Gulf Coast as a stand-alone project not requiring a Presidential Permit—a decision supported by the Obama administration. In April 2012, TransCanada submitted to Nebraska proposed pipeline routes avoiding the Sand Hills. Subsequently, on May 4, 2012, TransCanada submitted a new application for a Presidential Permit that includes proposed new routes through Nebraska. With the new permit application, the NEPA compliance process begins anew, although it may draw from relevant existing analysis and documentation prepared for the August 2011 final EIS.

In the wake of the State Department's denial of the Presidential Permit, Congress has debated legislative options addressing the Keystone XL pipeline. The Surface Transportation Extension Act of 2012, Part II (H.R. 4348) and the North American Energy Access Act (H.R. 3548) would transfer the permitting authority for the Keystone XL pipeline project to the Federal Energy Regulatory Commission, requiring FERC to issue a permit within 30 days of enactment. The Keystone For a Secure Tomorrow Act (H.R. 3811), the Grow America Act of 2012 (S. 2199), S. 2041 (a bill to approve the Keystone XL pipeline), the EXPAND Act (H.R. 4301), and the Energizing America through Employment Act (H.R. 4000) would immediately approve the original permit application filed by TransCanada. All seven bills include provisions allowing for later alteration of the pipeline route in Nebraska. S. 2100 and H.R. 4211 would suspend sales of petroleum products from the Strategic Petroleum Reserve until issuance of a Presidential Permit for the Keystone XL project. Changing or eliminating the State Department's role in issuing cross-border infrastructure permits may raise questions about the President's executive authority, however. H.R. 3900 would seek to ensure that crude oil transported by the Keystone XL pipeline, or resulting refined petroleum products, would be sold only into U.S. markets, but this bill could raise issues related to international trade agreements.

Contents

Figures

Tables

Appendixes

Contacts

Introduction[1]

In September 2008, TransCanada (a Canadian company) applied to the U.S. Department of State for a permit to cross the U.S.-Canada international border with the Keystone XL pipeline project. If constructed, the pipeline would carry crude oil produced from the oil sands region of Alberta, Canada, to U.S. Gulf Coast refineries. Because the pipeline would connect the United States with a foreign country, it requires a Presidential Permit issued by the State Department. Issuance of a Presidential Permit requires a finding that the project would serve the "national interest."

In the course of gathering information necessary to make its national interest determination, the State Department identified various concerns raised by the public. On November 10, 2011, the State Department announced its decision to seek additional information about alternative pipeline routes before it could move forward with a national interest determination.[2] More specifically, concerns regarding potential environmental impacts of constructing and operating the pipeline along the proposed route through the Sand Hills region of Nebraska led the State Department to decide that an assessment of potential alternative routes that would avoid that area was necessary. Subsequently, on November 14, 2011, TransCanada announced an agreement with the Nebraska Department of Environmental Quality to identify a pipeline route that would avoid the Sand Hills. The State Department estimated at the time that the preparation of supplemental environmental analysis necessary for a new route alternative could be complete in early 2013.

After the State Department's announcement of a delay in the permit review, Congress acted to expedite a permit decision on the Keystone XL project. The Temporary Payroll Tax Cut Continuation Act of 2011 (P.L. 112-78), enacted on December 23, 2011, included provisions requiring the Secretary of State to issue a permit for the project within 60 days, unless the President publicly determined the project not to be in the national interest. The act allowed for future changes to the Nebraska route if approved by the governor of Nebraska. On January 18, 2012, the State Department, with the President's consent, denied the Keystone XL permit, citing insufficient time under the 60-day deadline to obtain all the necessary information to assess the reconfigured project.[3]

On February 27, 2012, TransCanada announced that it would proceed with development of the Keystone XL segment connecting Cushing, OK, to the Gulf Coast as a stand-alone project not requiring a Presidential Permit.[4] The company also informed the State Department that it intended to file a new Presidential Permit application "in the near future" for the segment of the Keystone XL project from the Canadian border to Steele City, NE, with a future supplement to the application specifying an alternative route in Nebraska when that route is selected.[5]

---

[1] This report provides an overview of the Keystone XL project, permit review process, and general policy issues. For more detailed legal analysis, see CRS Report R42124, *Proposed Keystone XL Pipeline: Legal Issues*, by Adam Vann et al. For more analysis of U.S.-Canada energy trade, see CRS Report R41875, *The U.S.-Canada Energy Relationship: Joined at the Well*, by Paul W. Parfomak and Michael Ratner.

[2] U.S. Department of State, "Keystone XL Pipeline Project Review Process: Decision to Seek Additional Information," November 10, 2011, http://www.state.gov/r/pa/prs/ps/2011/11/176964 htm.

[3] U.S. Department of State, "Briefing on the Keystone XL Pipeline," briefing transcript, January 18, 2012, http://www.state.gov/r/pa/prs/ps/2012/01/181492.htm.

[4] TransCanada Corp., "TransCanada Set to Re-Apply for Keystone XL Permit Proceeding with Gulf Coast Project," press release, February 27, 2012.

[5] Ibid.

On May 4, 2012, the State Department received a new application from TransCanada for a proposed pipeline that would run from the Canadian border to connect to an existing pipeline in Steele City, NE.[6] The new application includes proposed new routes through Nebraska. The Obama administration has stated its support for TransCanada's plan to proceed with the southernmost segment of the Keystone XL pipeline, while reserving judgment on the reconfigured northern segment until completion of a new Presidential Permit review.[7]

Members of Congress have long expressed support for the proposed pipeline's potential energy security and economic benefits, while others have expressed reservations about its potential environmental impacts.[8] Though Congress, to date, has had no direct role in permitting the pipeline's construction, it may have an oversight role stemming from federal environmental statutes that govern the pipeline's application review process. Congress also may seek to influence the State Department permitting process, or may seek to assert direct congressional authority over permit approval, through new legislation.

A number of legislative proposals, like P.L. 112-78, would have imposed deadlines on a national interest determination for the Keystone XL project. The North American-Made Energy Security Act (H.R. 1938), would have directed the President to issue a final order granting or denying the Presidential Permit for the Keystone XL pipeline by November 1, 2011. The Jobs Through Growth Act (H.R. 3400), would have required the President to issue a final order granting or denying the Presidential Permit for the Keystone XL pipeline within 30 days of enactment. The North American Energy Security Act (S. 1932), which was introduced on November 30, 2011, would have required the Secretary of State to issue a permit for the project within 60 days of enactment, unless the President publicly determined the project to be not in the national interest. The North American Energy Security Act (H.R. 3537), introduced on December 1, 2011, and the Middle Class Tax Relief and Job Creation Act of 2011 (H.R. 3630), introduced on December 9, 2011, contain similar provisions for issuing a Presidential Permit within 60 days of enactment. All of these proposed provisions were mooted by the State Department's initial denial of the permit.

Provisions in the Surface Transportation Extension Act of 2012, Part II (H.R. 4348), which passed in the House on April 18, 2012, and in the North American Energy Access Act (H.R. 3548), introduced on December 2, 2011, would transfer the permitting authority over the Keystone XL pipeline project from the State Department to the Federal Energy Regulatory Commission (FERC), requiring the commission to issue a permit for the project within 30 days of enactment. The Keystone For a Secure Tomorrow Act (H.R. 3811), introduced on January 24, 2012, would immediately approve the original permit application filed by TransCanada in 2008. The Grow America Act of 2012 (S. 2199), introduced on March 15, 2012, the EXPAND Act (H.R. 4301), introduced on March 29, 2012, S. 2041 (a bill to approve the Keystone XL pipeline),

---

[6] See the State Department's "New Keystone XL Pipeline Project" webpage at http://www.keystonepipeline-xl.state.gov/.

[7] The White House, Office of the Press Secretary, "Statement by the Press Secretary," press release, February 27, 2012, http://www.whitehouse.gov/the-press-office/2012/02/27/statement-press-secretary.

[8] See, for example, Juliet Eilperin, "Democratic Lawmakers Pressure Obama Administration on Both Sides of Keystone Pipeline Issue," *Washington Post*, October 19, 2011; House Energy & Commerce Committee, Subcommittee on Energy and Power, Hearing on The American Energy Initiative, Discussion Draft of H.R. ____, the North American Made Energy Security Act of 2011, May 23, 2011; U.S. Senator Charles Grassley, Letter to Secretary of State Hillary Rodham Clinton, May 16, 2011; U.S. Senator Max Baucus, Letter to Secretary of State Hillary Rodham Clinton, September 10, 2010; U.S. Representative Henry A. Waxman, Letter to Secretary of State Hillary Rodham Clinton, July 2, 2010.

introduced on January 30, 2012, and the Energizing America through Employment Act (H.R. 4000), introduced on February 9, 2012, would similarly approve the original permit upon passage. All seven bills include provisions allowing for later alteration of the pipeline route in Nebraska.

H.R. 3900, introduced on February 3, 2012, would seek to ensure that any crude oil transported by the Keystone XL pipeline, or resulting refined petroleum products, would be sold only into U.S. markets—not exported overseas. S. 2100, introduced on February 13, 2012, and H.R. 4211, introduced on March 19, 2012, would suspend sales of petroleum products from the Strategic Petroleum Reserve until issuance of a Presidential Permit for the Keystone XL project application filed in 2008.

This report describes the Keystone XL pipeline proposal and the process required for federal approval. It summarizes key arguments for and against the pipeline put forth by the pipeline's developers, federal agencies, environmental groups, and other stakeholders. Finally, the report reviews the constitutional basis for the State Department's authority to issue a Presidential Permit, and opponents' possible challenges to this authority.

Pipeline Description

The U.S. portion of the Keystone XL pipeline project, as originally proposed, would pass through Montana, South Dakota, Nebraska, Oklahoma, and Texas (**Figure 1**). This route would consist of approximately 1,380 miles of 36-inch-diameter pipe and have the capacity to transport 830,000 barrels per day (bpd) of crude oil to the United States, delivering up to roughly 200,000 bpd to an existing oil terminal in Oklahoma with the remainder sent further to delivery points in Texas.[9] On November 14, 2011, TransCanada announced an agreement with the state of Nebraska to make as yet undetermined changes to the pipeline route in Nebraska to avoid environmentally sensitive areas.[10] These route changes are expected to increase the pipeline mileage through the state, although the company expects to maintain the original route through the other states, including its planned delivery points, so the pipeline's overall capacity should not be affected.

---

[9] U.S. Department of State, *Supplemental Draft Environmental Impact Statement for the Keystone XL Oil Pipeline Project,* April 15, 2011. p. 1-4. An initial capacity of 700,000 bpd may be raised to 830,000 bpd by increasing the pumping capacity. The Keystone XL project had applied to the Pipeline and Hazardous Materials Safety Administration to operate at slightly higher pressure than permitted in standard regulations, which would have enabled a 900,000 bpd capacity, but it withdrew its applications for such a Special Permit in August, 2010. The company may reapply for this exemption in the future, however, even after the pipeline is constructed, should it be approved.

[10] TransCanada Corp., "Media Advisory - State of Nebraska to Play Major Role in Defining New Keystone XL Route Away From the Sandhills," press release, November 14, 2011.

Figure 1. TransCanada Keystone Pipeline and Original Keystone XL Proposed Route

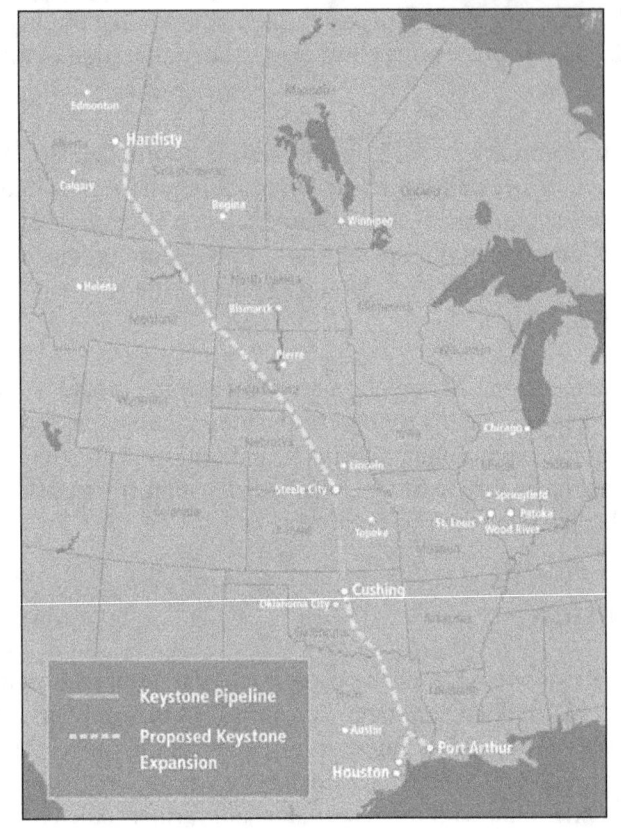

Source: U.S. Department of State, http://keystonepipeline-xl.state.gov/clientsite/keystonexl.nsf/map.jpg? OpenFileResource.

Note: Figure 1 shows the developer's originally proposed "preferred alternative" for the Keystone XL pipeline route according to Presidential Permit application documents. However, the route through Nebraska will change. For discussion of alternative routes, see the State Department EIS discussed below and **Figure 2**.

As of February 2011, the Keystone XL project along its original route was estimated to cost more than $7.0 billion, with the U.S. portion accounting for at least $5.4 billion of that total.[11] That is higher than the cost estimate when the initial permit application was filed, reportedly due to currency swings, changing regulatory requirements, and permitting delays.[12] A new route would presumably be longer and cost more. The Keystone XL pipeline would be an extension of TransCanada's existing Keystone pipeline, which links the Alberta oil sands to refineries in Illinois and Oklahoma (**Figure 1**). The Keystone pipeline received State Department approval on March 17, 2008, and began commercial operation in June 2010.

---

[11] TransCanada Keystone Pipeline, L.P., Application of TransCanada Keystone Pipeline L.P. for a Presidential Permit Authorizing the Construction, Operation, and Maintenance of Pipeline Facilities for the Importation of Crude Oil to be Located at the United States-Canada Border, U.S. Dept. of State, September 19, 2008, p. 10, http://www.keystonepipeline-xl.state.gov/clientsite/keystonexl nsf/presidentialpermitapplication.pdf? OpenFileResource.

[12] "TransCanada Expects $1-Billion Cost Escalation for Keystone XL Pipeline," Canadian Press, February 17, 2011.

Keystone XL Extension to Bakken Oil Production

The U.S. portion of the Bakken formation is an unconventional oil resource that underlies parts of North Dakota and Montana.[13] By the end of 2010, U.S. Bakken production was 350,000 bpd.[14] Output has climbed further since then. The oil is transported to refineries by rail and truck, rather than by pipeline, which would be more economic. In part, this is because infrastructure has not kept up with rapid production growth in the Bakken region in recent years. Output is expected to increase significantly in the future, increasing the need for pipeline transportation capacity.[15]

TransCanada has signed contracts with Bakken oil producers to carry 65,000 bpd from the region via the Keystone XL pipeline. While not the full 100,000 bpd of capacity TransCanada had offered to oil producers, this was enough to justify adding the Bakken Marketlink Project, a pipeline running from Baker, MT, to the Keystone XL pipeline, which can then carry crude to the oil hub at Cushing, OK and on to the Gulf Coast.[16] The Bakken Marketlink would have a 100,000 bpd capacity and is estimated to cost $140 million.[17]

These new Bakken contracts also improve the economics for Keystone XL, raising the amount of oil slated to flow through the pipeline.[18] Lower transportation costs and access to new markets may support investment in the Bakken. Furthermore, TransCanada is not the only company adding pipeline capacity in the region. Notably, Enbridge, another Canadian pipeline company, has proposed the Bakken Pipeline Project, which will add 120,000 bpd of transport capacity to move Bakken oil to Midwest markets.[19] According to Enbridge, sufficient pipeline capacity has been slow to emerge in the region because "they're smaller players in the Bakken. They are not able to make the 20-year commitments and it's been a lot of work to get them to commit to the level that [is] required to underwrite a major project out of the Bakken."[20] Rail transport capacity is also expanding.[21]

---

[13] Richard M. Pollastro et al., Assessment of Undiscovered Oil Resources in the Devonian-Mississippian Bakken Formation, Williston Basin Province, Montana and North Dakota, 2008, U.S. Geologic Survey, National Assessment of Oil and Gas Fact Sheet (2008–3021), April 2008, p. 1, http://pubs.usgs.gov/fs/2008/3021/pdf/FS08-3021_508.pdf. The Bakken formation also stretches into parts of Manitoba and Saskatchewan, Canada.

[14] Nathan Vanderklippe, "TransCanada to Move U.S. Crude Through Keystone," *The Globe and Mail*, January 26, 2011.

[15] For more on Bakken oil production, see CRS Report R42032, *The Bakken Formation: An Emerging Unconventional Oil Resource*, by Michael Ratner et al.

[16] Jeffrey Jones, "TransCanada Plans U.S. Bakken Pipeline Link," *Reuters*, January 20, 2011.

[17] TransCanada, "TransCanada to Transport U.S. Crude Oil to Market Bakken Open Season a Success," press release, January 11, 2011, http://www.transcanada.com/5631.html.

[18] Vanderklippe, 2011.

[19] Enbridge, "Bakken Pipeline Project—Project Overview," press release, http://www.enbridge.com/ BakkenPipelineProjects/BakkenPipelineProjectUS.aspx.

[20] Lauren Krugel, "TransCanada attracts support for Montana-to-Oklahoma crude pipeline," *The Canadian Press*, January 20, 2011.

[21] Selam Gebrekidan, "Bakken Rail Terminal Ships First Crude Cargo-Lario," *Reuters*, November 9, 2011.

Presidential Permit Application Requirements

Ordinarily, federal agencies have no authority to site oil pipelines, even interstate pipelines.[22] The primary siting authority for oil pipelines generally would be established under applicable state law (which may vary considerably from state to state). However, the construction, connection, operation, and maintenance of a pipeline that connects the United States with a foreign country requires executive permission conveyed through a Presidential Permit. Since the Keystone and proposed Keystone XL pipelines are designed for the importation of oil from Canada, their facilities require a Presidential Permit.

Executive Order 13337 delegates to the Secretary of State the President's authority to receive applications for Presidential Permits.[23] Issuance of a Presidential Permit is dependant upon a finding that the project would serve the "national interest." In the course of making that determination, the State Department is obligated to consider a host of issues related to the proposed project. The State Department will not necessarily evaluate the same factors for each project seeking a permit. However, the State Department identified the following as key factors it considered in making previous national interest determinations for pipeline permit applications:

- Environmental impacts of the proposed projects;

- Impacts of the proposed projects on the diversity of supply to meet U.S. crude oil demand and energy needs;

- The security of transport pathways for crude oil supplies to the United States through import facilities constructed at the border relative to other modes of transport;

- Stability of trading partners from whom the United States obtains crude oil;

- Relationship between the United States and various foreign suppliers of crude oil and the ability of the United States to work with those countries to meet overall environmental and energy security goals;

- Impact of proposed projects on broader foreign policy objectives, including a comprehensive strategy to address climate change;

- Economic benefits to the United States of constructing and operating proposed projects; and

- Relationships between proposed projects and goals to reduce reliance on fossil fuels and to increase use of alternative and renewable energy sources.[24]

---

[22] This is in contrast to interstate natural gas pipelines, which, under Section 7(c) (15 USC §717f(c)) of the Natural Gas Act, must obtain a "certificate of public convenience and necessity" from the Federal Energy Regulatory Commission.

[23] See Executive Order 13337, "Issuance of Permits With Respect to Certain Energy-Related Facilities and Land Transportation Crossings on the International Boundaries of the United States," 69 *Federal Register* 25299, May 5, 2004, as amended, and Department of State Delegation of Authority No. 118-2 of January 26, 2006. The source of Permitting Authority for relevant Executive Orders is discussed further in the **Appendix A**.

[24] This list was included in the State Department's *Final Environmental Impact Statement for the Keystone Xl Project* under a discussion regarding the Presidential Permit Review Process (p. 1-4). It was noted that this list is not exhaustive, and that the State Department may consider additional factors in its national interest determination process.

In making its national interest determination, the State Department is required to consult with relevant federal and state agencies and to invite public comment in arriving at its determination. However, the State Department has broad discretion in determining what factors it will examine to inform its determination and, ultimately, whether a proposed project is in the national interest.

Documenting Environmental Impacts Under NEPA

As identified on the list above, a proposed project's environmental impacts is one factor considered by the State Department in making its national interest determination. The State Department's identification and consideration of environmental impacts is documented within the context of preparing an Environmental Impact Statement (EIS), pursuant to the National Environmental Policy Act (NEPA, 42 U.S.C. §4321 et seq.).[25]

Broadly, NEPA requires federal agencies to consider the environmental impacts of their actions before proceeding with them and to inform the public of those potential impacts. To ensure that environmental impacts are considered, an EIS must be prepared for major federal actions "significantly" affecting the environment.[26] With respect to the 2008 Presidential Permit application submitted by TransCanada, the State Department concluded that issuance of a permit for the proposed construction, connection, operation, and maintenance of the Keystone XL Pipeline and its associated facilities at the United States border would constitute a major federal action that may have a significant impact upon the environment within the meaning of NEPA.[27] For this reason, the State Department prepared an EIS to address reasonably foreseeable impacts from the proposed action and alternatives. Similarly, an EIS will have to be prepared for pipeline project for which the May 4, 2012, permit application was filed.

Overview of the NEPA Process for the XL Pipeline Project

Among other requirements, an EIS must include a statement of the purpose and need for an action, a description of all reasonable alternatives to meet that purpose and need, a description of the environment to be affected by those alternatives, and an analysis of the direct and indirect effects of the alternatives, including cumulative impacts.[28] Accordingly, the State Department EIS must demonstrate the review and consider potential environmental impacts of the entire pipeline

---

[25] In processing Presidential Permit applications, the State Department is also explicitly directed to review the project's compliance with the National Historic Preservation Act (16 U.S.C. §470f), the Endangered Species Act (16 U.S.C. §1531 et seq.), and Executive Order 12898 of February 11, 1994 (59 *Federal Register* 7629), concerning environmental justice. In processing the permit application for the Keystone XL Pipeline project, issues associated with NEPA compliance have drawn the most attention. In large part, that is likely because it is during the NEPA process that compliance with these, as well as any other environmental requirements, would be identified, documented, and demonstrated.

[26] 42 U.S.C. §4332(2)(C).

[27] U.S. Department of State, "Notice of Intent to Prepare an Environmental Impact Statement and to Conduct Scoping Meetings and Notice of Floodplain and Wetland Involvement and to Initiate Consultation under Section 106 of the National Historic Preservation Act for the Proposed TransCanada Keystone XL Pipeline," 74 *Federal Register* 5020, January 28, 2009.

[28] In preparing an EIS associated with a Presidential Permit, NEPA regulations promulgated by both the Council of Environmental Quality (CEQ) and the State Department would apply. CEQ regulations implementing NEPA (under 40 C.F.R. §§1500-1508) apply to all federal agencies. NEPA regulations applicable to State Department actions, which supplement the CEQ regulations, are found at 22 C.F.R. §161.

(including the construction, operation, and maintenance of the pipeline and its associated facilities), not just the facilities at the border crossing.

As the NEPA compliance process for TransCanada's permit application has proceeded, it is important to understand the distinction between what is required under NEPA itself and what may be required pursuant to other environmental requirements identified within the context of the NEPA process. NEPA itself requires federal agencies to identify the environmental impacts of an action before proceeding with them and to involve the public in that process when environmental impacts are significant. In that process of identifying a proposed project's environmental impacts, within the context of preparing the EIS, the lead agency should identify any compliance obligations (licenses, permits, or approvals) established under additional state, tribal and federal law applicable to the portion of the project constructed in the United States (see "State Siting and Additional Environmental Requirements," below).

EIS preparation is done in two stages, resulting in a draft and final EIS. NEPA regulations require the draft EIS to be circulated for public and agency comment, followed by a final EIS that incorporates those comments.[29] Preparing the EIS is the responsibility of a designated "lead agency," in this case, the State Department. In developing the EIS, the State Department must rely to some extent on information provided by TransCanada. For example, TransCanada's original permit application included an Environmental Report which was intended to provide the State Department with sufficient information to understand the scope of potential environmental impacts of the project.[30]

In preparing the draft EIS, the lead agency must request input from "cooperating agencies," which include any agency with jurisdiction by law or with special expertise regarding any environmental impact associated with the project.[31] Cooperating agencies for the Keystone XL project (for the pipeline's first Presidential Permit application) were the U.S. Environmental Protection Agency (EPA); the Department of Transportation's Pipeline and Hazardous Materials Safety Administration (PHMSA), Office of Pipeline Safety (OPS); the Department of the Interior's Bureau of Land Management, U.S. Fish and Wildlife Service, and National Park Service; the U.S. Army Corps of Engineers; the U.S. Department of Agriculture's Farm Service Agency, Natural Resources Conservation Service, and Rural Utilities Service; the Department of Energy's Western Area Power Administration; and state environmental agencies.

In addition to its role as a cooperating agency, EPA is also required to review and comment publicly on the EIS and rate both the adequacy of the EIS itself and the level of environmental impact of the proposed project.[32] Rating the EIS takes place after the draft is issued. The EIS could be rated either "Adequate," "Insufficient Information," or "Inadequate." EPA's rating of a project's environmental impacts may range from "Lack of Objections" to "Environmentally

---

[29] For more analysis of NEPA requirements, see CRS Report RL33152, *The National Environmental Policy Act (NEPA): Background and Implementation,* by Linda Luther.

[30] Documents submitted for the initial 2008 Presidential Permit application have now been archived by the State Department. Documents related to that original application are available at http://keystonepipeline-xl.state.gov/archive/index htm.

[31] 40 C.F.R. §1508.5. Also, Executive Order 13337 directs the Secretary of State to refer an application for a Presidential Permit to other specifically identified federal departments and agencies on whether granting the application would be in the national interest.

[32] For more information, see the U.S. Environmental Protection Agency's "Environmental Impact Statement (EIS) Rating System Criteria" at http://www.epa.gov/compliance/nepa/comments/ratings html.

Unsatisfactory." In rating the impact of the action itself, EPA would specify one of the following: "Lack of Objections," "Environmental Concerns," "Environmental Objections," or "Environmentally Unsatisfactory." The federal agency would then be required to respond to EPA's rating, as appropriate.

EPA's role in rating draft EISs had a significant impact on the NEPA process for TransCanada's 2008 Presidential Permit application. Major milestones in that NEPA process are listed in **Table 1** (for more detail on the milestones listed, see **Appendix B**).

Table 1. NEPA Milestones for TransCanada's 2008 Presidential Permit Application

Administrative, Congressional, State, and Company Actions That Affected the NEPA Process

Date	Party	Description
Sept. 2008	TransCanada	An application for a Presidential Permit is filed with the State Department to build and operate the Keystone XL Project; a "Preliminary Environmental Report" for the project is also submitted.
Apr. 16, 2010	State Department	Draft EIS for the proposed Keystone XL Pipeline project is released for public comment.
July 16, 2010	EPA	The agency rates the draft EIS as "Inadequate," noting that potentially significant impacts were not evaluated, that the additional information and analysis was needed, and that the draft EIS would need to be formally revised and again made available for public review.
Oct. 21, 2010	State Department	Secretary Clinton states that the State Department was "inclined to" approve the project. Critics of the project, including some Members of Congress, stated that the Secretary's statement appeared to prejudge its permit approval for the pipeline proposal as a foregone conclusion.
Apr. 15, 2011	State Department	Supplemental draft EIS issued.
June 6, 2011	EPA	The agency rates the supplemental draft EIS as having "Insufficient Information" and the action as having "Environmental Objections." EPA recommends additional analysis on a range of issues.
Aug. 26, 2011	State Department	Final EIS issued.
Aug. - Oct. 2011	State Department	The 90-day public review period for National Interest Determination begins; State Department holds public meetings in the six states through which the proposed pipeline would pass and in Washington, D.C.
Oct. 2011	Congress	Fourteen Members of Congress request the State Department Office of Inspector General (IG) to investigate the department's handling of the EIS and National Interest Determination for the Keystone XL project.
Oct. 24, 2011	Governor of Nebraska	The Governor calls the Nebraska legislature into a special session to determine if siting legislation can be crafted and passed for pipeline routing in Nebraska.
Nov. 4, 2011	State Department	IG announces it is initiating a special review to determine to what extent the Department and all other parties involved complied with Federal laws and regulations relating to the Keystone XL pipeline permit process.
Nov. 10, 2011	State Department	The agency announces that additional information will be needed regarding alternative pipeline routes that would avoid the Nebraska Sand Hills before National Interest Determination can be made. Officials suggest that analysis needed to prepare the supplemental EIS, including additional public comment, could be completed as early as the first quarter of 2013.

Date	Party	Description
Nov. 14, 2011	TransCanada	The company announces that it will work with the Nebraska Department of Environmental Quality (DEQ) to identify a potential pipeline route that would avoid the Nebraska Sand Hills.
Nov. 22, 2011	Governor of Nebraska	The Governor signs legislation passed during the special session directing the Nebraska DEQ to work collaboratively with the State Department to gather information necessary for a supplemental EIS.
Nov. 2011	Nebraska DEQ/State Department	The agencies begin to negotiate a Memorandum of Understanding (MOU) regarding their collaboration on the supplemental EIS. Nebraska DEQ hires a contractor to delineate the "Sand Hills" region that alternative routes must avoid.
Dec. 23, 2011	Congress	The Temporary Payroll Tax Cut Continuation Act of 2011 (P.L. 112-78) is enacted, including provisions requiring the Secretary of State to issue a permit for the project within 60 days, unless the President determines the project is not in the national interest.
Jan. 18, 2012	State Department	The agency announces, with the President's consent, that it will deny the Keystone XL permit. It states that its decision was predicated on the fact that the 60-day deadline under P.L. 112-78 did not provide sufficient time to obtain information necessary to assess the current project's national interest.
Feb. 3, 2012	State Department	Formal permit denial issued; State Department and Nebraska DEQ suspend work on MOU regarding a supplemental EIS.
Feb. 9, 2012	State Department	The IG releases findings reporting that the State Department "did not violate its role as an unbiased oversight agency," among other specific findings regarding department's Keystone XL permit review process.
Apr. 19, 2012	TransCanada	The company submits to the Nebraska DEQ an initial analysis of alternative Keystone XL pipeline routes that avoid the Sand Hills.
May 4, 2012	TransCanada	A new Presidential Permit application is submitted to State Department reflecting new information regarding alternative pipeline routes through Nebraska. The NEPA process for the new project begins, potentially drawing upon relevant documents from the 2011 final EIS.

Source: The Congressional Research Service, based on a review of events during, and affecting, the NEPA process conducted for the 2008 Presidential permit application for the Keystone XL pipeline project.

As illustrated in **Table 1**, following the release of the Keystone XL project's final EIS, a public review period began during which the proposed project's national interest determination could be made. As part of this process for the initial Keystone XL project, the State Department held public meetings in each of the six states through which the proposed pipeline would pass and in Washington, DC.[33] The meetings were intended to give members of the public additional opportunity to voice their opinions on issues they thought should be taken into account in determining whether granting or denying the Presidential Permit would be in the national interest. These additional public meetings were not part of the NEPA process. Considering the strong public interest in the pipeline proposal (both opposed and in favor), the public hearings were part of the State Department's national interest determination. During the review period, the State Department received input from state, local, and tribal officials as well as members of the public.

[33] U.S. Department of State press release, "Keystone XL Final Environmental Impact Statement Released; Public Meetings Set," August 26, 2011, http://www.state.gov/r/pa/prs/ps/2011/08/171082 htm.

On November 10, 2011, after the public review period, the State Department issued a statement regarding the public comments and its response to those comments.[34] The State Department stated that it received comments on a wide range of issues including the Keystone XL project's potential impact on jobs, pipeline safety, health concerns, the societal impact of the project, and oil extraction in Canada. Concern regarding the proposed pipeline route through the Sand Hills area of Nebraska was identified as one of the most common issues raised. Comments regarding that pipeline route were consistent with the environmental impacts identified in the final EIS with regard to the unique combination of characteristics of the Sand Hills region (e.g., a high concentration of wetlands of special concern, a sensitive ecosystem, and extensive areas of very shallow groundwater). Further, the Nebraska legislature was convening a special session to consider the legislation that would establish regulations applicable to pipeline siting within the state.

Facing the prospect of new state pipeline siting regulations applicable to the Sand Hills, together with the concern about the Keystone XL pipeline's specific "preferred" route, the State Department announced that it needed additional information about alternative pipeline routes avoiding the environmentally sensitive Sand Hills area in Nebraska before moving forward with its national interest determination.[35] Although the State Department did not decide that environmental issues led to a determination that the proposed project was not in the national interest, environmental issues identified in the final EIS, and further stressed in public comments, led to its decision to delay that determination until it gathered this information. In a concurrent press release, President Obama stated

> Because this permit decision could affect the health and safety of the American people as well as the environment, and because a number of concerns have been raised through a public process, we should take the time to ensure that all questions are properly addressed and all the potential impacts are properly understood.[36]

Subsequently, TransCanada announced that it would work with the State Department and the Nebraska Department of Environmental Quality (DEQ) to conduct an environmental assessment to define the best location for Keystone XL pipeline in Nebraska. Further, the company stated that it would "cooperate with these agencies and provide them with the information they need to complete a thorough review that addresses concerns regarding the Sandhills region."[37]

The Role of Environmental Impacts in a National Interest Determination

Generally, after a final EIS is issued for a pipeline project that requires a Presidential Permit, a final project decision would be reflected in a "Record of Decision and National Interest Determination," issued by the State Department.[38] That document, required under elements of both NEPA and E.O. 11424, formalizes the selection of a project alternative.

---

[34] U.S. Department of State, "Keystone XL Pipeline Project Review Process: Decision to Seek Additional Information," Media Note, PRN 2011/1909, Office of the Spokesperson, November 10, 2011.

[35] U.S. Department of State, November 10, 2011, see footnote 34.

[36] The White House, Office of the Press Secretary, "Statement by the President on the State Department's Keystone XL Pipeline Announcement," November 10, 2011.

[37] See TransCanada Corp., Media Advisory, "State of Nebraska to Play Major Role in Defining New Keystone XL Route Away From the Sandhills," November 14, 2011, available at http://www.transcanada.com/5896.html.

[38] For example, see U.S. Department of State, *Record of Decision and National Interest Determination, TransCanada* (continued...)

However, after the 90-day public review period, instead of issuing that final decision document, the State Department announced its decision to gather additional information regarding the alternative pipeline routes. This scenario illustrates the distinctly different, yet interrelated requirements applicable to NEPA process, that culminates with the publication of a final record of decision (ROD) and the national interest determination that is necessary under E.O. 13337 (as amended). Under NEPA, the State Department (or any other federal agency considering an action) must fully assess the environmental consequences of an action and potential project alternatives *before* making a final decision. NEPA does not prohibit a federal action that has adverse environment impacts; it requires only that a federal agency be fully *aware of* and *consider* those adverse impacts before selecting a final project alternative. That is, NEPA is intended to be part of the decision-making process, not dictate a particular outcome. The State Department's national interest determination decision, however, does dictate a particular outcome—issuance of a Presidential Permit. That is, issuance of a Presidential Permit is predicated on the Secretary of State finding that the proposed project would serve the national interest. While NEPA does not prohibit federal actions with adverse environmental impacts, a project's adverse environmental impacts (as well as other factors) may lead the State Department to determine that it is not in the national interest.

Although no new decision deadline was established, State Department officials suggested that it would be "reasonable to expect that this process including a public comment period on a supplement to the final EIS consistent with NEPA could be completed as early as the first quarter of 2013."[39] In a prior press interview, President Obama also appeared to suggest that, notwithstanding the delegation of Presidential Permit authority to the State Department, he would be personally involved in the final decision on the Keystone XL Pipeline permit application.[40]

Presidential Permit Denial

As noted earlier, on December 23, 2011, the Temporary Payroll Tax Cut Continuation Act of 2011 was enacted (P.L. 112-78). Under Section 501, "Permit for Keystone XL pipeline," the Secretary of State was required to grant the Presidential Permit for the Keystone XL pipeline project within 60 days, unless the President determined that the pipeline would not be in the national interest. On January 18, 2012, the State Department announced, with the President's concurrence, that the Presidential Permit for the proposed Keystone XL Pipeline would be denied at that time because it was determined not to serve the national interest. That recommendation "was predicated on the fact that the Department does not have sufficient time to obtain the information necessary to assess whether the project, in its current state, is in the national interest."[41] However, the department also stated that its decision did not preclude TransCanada from reapplying for a Presidential Permit in the future.

(...continued)

Keystone Pipeline, LP Application for Presidential Permit, February 25, 2008, http://www.cardnoentrix.com/keystone/project/SignedROD.pdf.

[39] U.S. Department of State, November 10, 2011, footnote 34.

[40] KETV NewsWatch 7, "Uncut: KETV's Rob McCartney Interviews President Obama," Omaha, NE, November 1, 2011, http://www.ketv.com/video/29652519/detail.html.

[41] U.S. Department of State, Media Note, "Denial of the Keystone XL Pipeline Application," January 18, 2012, available at http://www.state.gov/r/pa/prs/ps/2012/01/181473 htm.

The State Department announcement reiterated the concerns regarding the proposed route through the Sand Hills area of Nebraska and the need for additional information regarding alternative routes around that region before it could make a national interest determination. As it had previously, the State Department estimated that, based on prior projects of similar length and scope and after consultations with the State of Nebraska and TransCanada, it could complete the necessary review to make a decision by the first quarter of 2013.

In a briefing following the State Department permit denial, it was noted that a new permit application would trigger a new environmental review process under NEPA.[42] It was further noted, however, that regulations under both NEPA and the State Department internal procedures allow for the use of relevant, existing NEPA documentation and analysis. The final EIS completed in August 2011, as well as the body of information gathered to prepare that document, could potentially be used to prepare required NEPA documentation for a new permit application. The degree to which the previous documentation would be useful would depend on the degree to which the previously proposed Keystone XL pipeline would be similar to a newly proposed pipeline project.

On February 27, 2012, in the wake of the Presidential Permit denial, TransCanada advised the State Department of its intent to file a Presidential Permit application in the near future and subsequently supplement that application with an alternative route in Nebraska, as soon as that route is selected by the state.[43] (The company began work on developing alternative routes that would avoid the Sand Hills shortly after the State Department's November 11th announcement that it would need more information about alternative routes as a condition of making its national interest determination.) TransCanada also advised the State Department that it would proceed with development of the pipeline segment connecting Cushing, OK, to the Gulf Coast as a stand-alone project (the Gulf Coast Pipeline Project) entirely within the United States. As a project that does not involve an international border crossing, a Presidential Permit will not be required for the Gulf Coast leg of the project. However, as a pipeline carrying a hazardous material, it will still be required to comply with a range of state and federal permit, approval, and consultation requirements (see "State Siting and Additional Environmental Requirements").

The New Permit Application Process

On April 19, 2012, the Nebraska DEQ received TransCanada's *Initial Report Identifying Alternative and Preferred Corridors for Nebraska Reroute* route.[44] Public meetings on the newly proposed routes were scheduled for May 9-17. On May 4, 2012, TransCanada submitted a new application for authorization for a Presidential Permit authorizing the constructions, connection, operations and maintenance of pipeline facilities for the importation of crude oil at the United State-Canada border. The new Keystone XL pipeline project would cross the border at Phillips County, MT, and extend to a point on the existing Keystone pipeline system at Steel City, NE. The changes to the route involve only the segment through Nebraska.

---

[42] U.S. State Department, Kerri-Ann Jones, Assistant Secretary, Bureau of Oceans and International Environmental and Scientific Affairs, "Briefing on the Keystone XL Pipeline," January 18, 2012, transcript available at http://www.state.gov/r/pa/prs/ps/2012/01/181492.htm.

[43] TransCanada Corp. press release, "TransCanada Set to Re-Apply for Keystone XL Permit Proceeding with Gulf Coast Project," February 27, 2012, available at http://www.transcanada.com/5966 html.

[44] See Nebraska DEQ's webpage "Nebraska Keystone XL Pipeline Evaluation: NDEQ's Role in the Pipeline Review Process" https://ecmp.nebraska.gov/deq-seis/.

As with other Presidential Permit applications, the State Department asserted its need to determine if granting a permit for the proposed pipeline is in the national interest. Consistent with E.O. 13337, that determination will involve the consideration of factors, including energy security, health, environmental, cultural, economic, and foreign policy concerns. To do so, the Department stated that it would select an independent third-party contractor to assist in that process, including a review of the existing EIS from the previous Keystone XL pipeline permit process, as well as identifying and assisting with new analysis.[45] Also, the State Department reaffirmed that it would cooperate with the state of Nebraska, as well as other relevant state and federal agencies, in the review of the application. Finally, the department acknowledged that Nebraska officials expect their review of the new proposed route to take six to nine months. As a result, the State Department estimates that it would complete the review process in the first quarter of 2013.

State Siting and Additional Environmental Requirements

As stated above, the federal government does not currently exercise siting authority over oil pipelines. Instead, siting for the Keystone XL pipeline must comply with any applicable state law—which can vary from state to state. South Dakota, for example, required TransCanada to apply for a permit for the Keystone XL pipeline from the state public utility commission, which issued the permit on April 25, 2010.[46] Montana requires a certificate from the state's Department of Environmental Quality.[47]

At the time of TransCanada's application for a Presidential Permit, Nebraska did not have any permitting requirements that applied specifically to the construction and operation of oil pipelines, although a state statute does include an "eminent domain" provision, which grants eminent domain authority to oil pipeline companies that are unable to obtain the necessary property rights from the relevant property owners.[48] However, due to the controversy surrounding the Keystone XL project, the Nebraska Governor called a special session of its legislature to enact legislation to assert state authority over pipeline siting. Subsequently, the state enacted two laws—one that would affect the siting of the Keystone XL pipeline (see **Table 1**) and one that outlines procedures for siting any future oil pipeline in Nebraska.[49] The latter will require oil pipeline carrier proposing to construct a major oil pipeline in Nebraska to file an application with the state's Public Service Commission and receive approval before beginning construction. Additionally, the law authorized the Commission to follow certain procedures before deciding whether a proposed oil pipeline would serve the public interest.

Although there are limited federal requirements applicable to oil pipeline *siting*, there are numerous local, state, tribal, and federal requirements applicable to pipeline construction,

---

[45] See the State Department's "New Keystone XL Pipeline Project" webpage at http://www.keystonepipeline-xl.state.gov/.

[46] South Dakota Public Utilities Commission, Final Decision and Order; Notice of Entry Before the Public Utilities Commission of the State of South Dakota, In the Matter of the Application by Transcanada Keystone Pipeline, LP for a Permit Under the South Dakota Energy Conversion and Transmission Facilities Act to Construct the Keystone Pipeline Project, HP07-001, http://puc.sd.gov/commission/orders/HydrocarbonPipeline/2008/hp07-001.pdf.

[47] Montana Major Facility Siting Act, Title 75, Chapter 20.

[48] Nebraska Rev. Stat. §57-1101.

[49] See Nebraska Governor Dave Heineman's November 23, 2011 statement "Common Sense Solution," available at http://www.governor.nebraska.gov/columns/2011/11/23_solution.html.

operation, and maintenance. For example, the August 2011 final EIS for the Keystone XL pipeline identified a list of permits, licenses, approvals and consultation that would be required before the pipeline project could proceed.[50] From that list, following are a few of the requirements that would likely apply to any pipeline project, listed by agency with jurisdiction over that requirement:

- The U.S. Army Corps of Engineers—issuance of a permit for sections of the project that require placement of dredge and fill material in waters of the United States, including wetlands (pursuant to Section 404 of the Clean Water Act), or for pipeline crossings of navigable waters (pursuant to Section 10 of the Rivers and Harbors Act);

- The Environmental Protection Agency—review and issue National Pollutant Discharge Elimination System permits for the discharge of pollutants in state waters (pursuant to Section 402 of the Clean Water Act);

- The Bureau of Land Management—grant temporary use permits for portions of the project that would encroach on federal lands;

- U.S. Fish and Wildlife Service—consider impacts to federally listed endangered species (pursuant to the Endangered Species Act) and provide a Biological Opinion if the project is likely to adversely affect federally listed species.

- Multiple state/county agencies—consult on and/or consider issuance of permits for projects that cross navigable waters or state highways, or involve work potentially affecting state streams, cultural resources, or natural resources.

The time it takes to complete the NEPA process has been a focus of attention for the first Presidential Permit application for the Keystone XL pipeline. However, for past pipeline projects, obtaining all required local, state, tribal, and federal permits, approvals, and licenses may take a similar amount of time. By way of example, for the Alberta Clipper pipeline project, another oil sands pipeline, the Presidential Permit process (i.e., completion of the NEPA process and the national interest determination and issuance of a permit) took approximately two years. Obtaining the necessary permits, approvals, and licenses for construction of the pipeline took an additional two years.

Legislative Efforts to Change Permitting Authority

In light of the State Department's denial of the Keystone XL permit, some in Congress have sought alternative means to support development of the pipeline. As stated in the Introduction, there are a number of legislative proposals to change the federal permitting authority for the pipeline. Key among these is the Surface Transportation Extension Act of 2012, Part II (H.R. 4348), which passed in the House on April 18, 2012. This bill (and H.R. 3548) would transfer the permitting authority over the Keystone XL pipeline project from the State Department to the Federal Energy Regulatory Commission (FERC), requiring the commission to issue a permit for the project within 30 days of enactment. Other proposals, such as H.R. 3811, would directly shift permitting authority to Congress, approving the original permit application filed by TransCanada in 2008 upon enactment.

---

[50] Keystone XL pipeline project final EIS, "Introduction: Section 1.10. Permits, Approvals, and Regulatory Requirements," Table 1.10-1.

Changing, or eliminating altogether, the State Department's role in issuing cross-border infrastructure permits may raise questions about the President's executive authority (further discussed in the **Appendix A**). In response to H.R. 3548, for example, the State Department's key official on Keystone XL testified before Congress:

> The legislation raises serious questions about existing legal authorities, questions the continuing force of much of the federal and all of the state and local environmental and land use management authority over the pipeline, and overrides foreign policy and national security considerations implicated by a cross border permit, which are properly assessed by the State Department.[51]

Such proposals may also raise some administrative and legal challenges for FERC or other federal agencies. A senior FERC official testified that a proposal like H.R. 3548 does not provide enough time for an "adequate" public record, provides no clear authority for enforcing measures required in the EIS, does not articulate a process for authorizing alterations to the pipeline route in Nebraska, and is unclear about permits required from other federal agencies, among other concerns.[52] For additional analysis of associated legal issues, see CRS Report R42124, *Proposed Keystone XL Pipeline: Legal Issues*, by Adam Vann et al.

Given the State Department's initial permit denial, and opposition from various environmental groups and stakeholders along the pipeline route, legal challenges are a possibility. However, in the event of a challenge based on an environmental issue, the distinction between State Department actions required under NEPA and those required under its authority to issue a Presidential Permit would be relevant. NEPA does not create a private right of action. Instead, judicial challenges to a federal agency action under NEPA are brought pursuant to the Administrative Procedure Act (APA, 5 U.S.C. §§706 et seq.). Presidential actions, however, are not subject to judicial review under the APA.[53] That is, the final agency action reflected in a ROD is subject to judicial review, but the State Department's national interest determination, made under its authority to issue a Presidential Permit, is not. For more information regarding the State Department's authority to grant a Presidential Permit, see the **Appendix A.**

Arguments For and Against the Pipeline

Proponents of the Keystone XL pipeline, including Canadian agencies and U.S. and Canadian petroleum industry stakeholders, base their arguments supporting the pipeline primarily on increasing the diversity of the U.S. petroleum supply and economic benefits to the United States, especially job creation. Opponents to the pipeline are generally environmental organizations and community groups. Their concerns stem from issues that can be broadly categorized as the

---

[51] Kerri-Ann Jones, Assistant Secretary of State for Oceans and International Environmental and Scientific Affairs, Testimony before the House Energy and Commerce Committee, Subcommittee on Energy and Power Hearing on the North American Energy Access Act, January 25, 2012.

[52] Jeff Wright, Director, Office of Energy Projects, Federal Energy Regulatory Commission, Testimony before the House Energy and Commerce Committee, Subcommittee on Energy and Power Hearing on the North American Energy Access Act, January 25, 2012.

[53] While the APA's definition of "agency" does not specifically exclude or include the president, the Supreme Court has held that exercises of presidential authority are not subject to judicial review because the president is not an agency (*Dalton v. Specter*, 511 U.S. 462, 470 (1994)). The Court has also held that the APA does not apply to the president based on separation of powers principles (*Franklin v. Massachusetts*, 505 U.S. 788, 800-01 (1992)).

pipeline's global or domestic impacts. "Global" impacts stem primarily from concern regarding the lifecycle greenhouse gas (GHG) emissions associated with the development and extraction of Canadian oil sands, compared to conventional oil or renewable fuels. Although the concern regarding GHG emissions is focused primarily on the extraction process, opponents also argue that use of the oil sands crude promotes continued U.S. dependency on fossil fuels. Concern over adverse domestic impacts of the pipeline stem primarily from impacts associated with the pipeline's construction and long-term use on private land—particularly its potential to affect agricultural uses and cattle grazing. Communities along the pipeline route are also concerned about the risk of a potential release of heavy crude and the operators' ability to respond to a release, particularly in remote areas.

Impacts to the Nebraska Sand Hills

In the process of examining factors necessary to determine whether the Presidential Permit for the original Keystone XL pipeline route was in the national interest, the State Department decided that it needed to assess potential alternative pipeline routes that would avoid the Sand Hills region of Nebraska. Unique characteristics of the Sand Hills, including its high concentration of wetlands, extensive areas of very shallow groundwater, and its sensitive ecosystem, were identified as factors that resulted in increasing public concern over the proposed pipeline location. For these reasons, TransCanada announced it would work with the Nebraska Department of Environmental Quality to identify a potential pipeline route that would avoid the Sand Hills.

To understand the concerns associated with potential environmental impacts of the construction and operation of a pipeline that crosses the Sand Hills (also referred to as the Sandhills), an understanding of the unique size and structure of the region is useful. The Sand Hills region is a 19,600 square mile sand dune formation stabilized by native grasslands that cover 95% of its surface. The surface is highly susceptible to wind erosion if the grassland is disturbed.[54] Below its surface lie hundreds of feet of course sand and gravel. Essentially, the porous soil acts like a giant sponge that quickly absorbs precipitation, allowing very little to run off. In some areas, the water table reaches the land surface—a characteristic that creates lakes that dot the region as well as 1.3 million acres of wetlands. The loose, porous soil and sensitivity to wind erosion have been factors contributing to a lack of development on the Sand Hills. As a result, the region contains the most intact natural habitat of the Great Plains of the United States. The porosity of the soil is also relevant because the Sand Hills sits atop the Ogallala Aquifer—one of the largest aquifer systems in the world.[55]

The highly porous soil of the Sand Hills make it a significant recharge zone in the northern region of the Ogallala Aquifer system. That is, the sandy, porous soil of the Sand Hills allows a significant amount of surface water to enter (recharge) the aquifer system. Water from the aquifer also accounts for a significant amount of water use—78% of the region's public water, 83% of irrigation water in Nebraska, and 30% of water used in the United States for irrigation and agriculture.

---

[54] For more information, see the Department of the Interior's U.S. Fish and Wildlife Service web page on the Sand Hills at http://www.fws.gov/mountain-prairie/pfw/ne/ne4 htm.

[55] The entire Ogallala Aquifer system stretches across eight states generally from north to south to include South Dakota, Nebraska, Wyoming, Colorado, Kansas, Oklahoma, New Mexico, and Texas and underlies about 174,000 square miles.

Potential impacts to the Ogallala Aquifer and the Sand Hills identified in the final EIS for TransCanada's original permit application included potential groundwater contamination after a release (e.g., a spill or leak from a hole or damaged portion of the pipeline) of crude oil during the construction or operation of the proposed pipeline. Along the preferred route of the originally proposed pipeline configuration, areas in the Sand Hills region were identified as locations where the water table may be close to the surface. The depth to groundwater was less than 10 feet for approximately 65 miles of the preferred pipeline route in Nebraska. Both the soil porosity and the close proximity of groundwater to the surface increase the potential that a release of oil from the pipeline could contaminate groundwater in the region.[56]

The new route alternative TransCanada has proposed for the Nebraska section of the Keystone XL pipeline avoids the Sand Hills (**Figure 2**). However, the pipeline would still cross part of the Ogallala aquifer.

Figure 2. Keystone XL Preferred Alternative Route in Nebraska

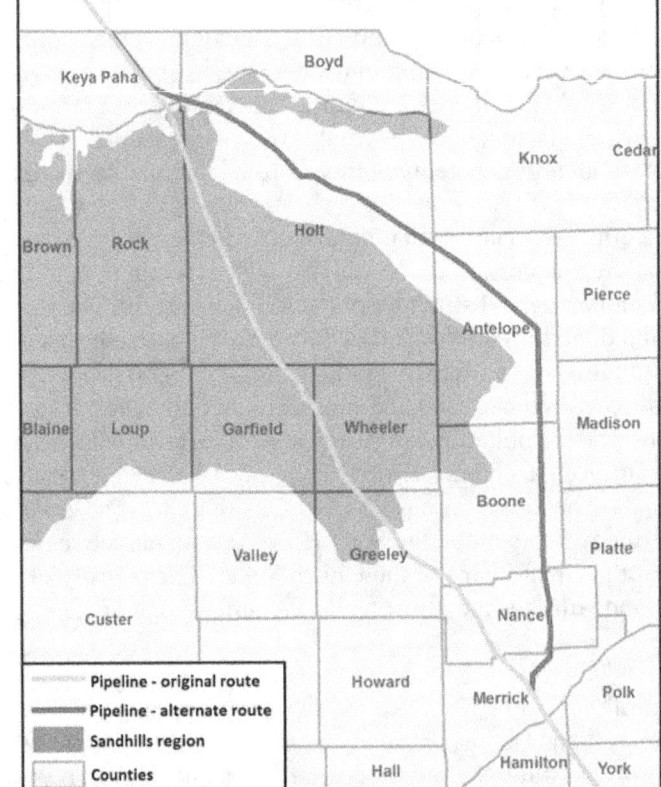

Source: Congressional Research Service, adapted from TransCanada, *TransCanada Keystone XL Pipeline Project, Initial Report Identifying Alternative and Preferred Corridors for Nebraska Reroute*, April 18, 2012, http://www.eenews.net/assets/2012/04/19/document_cw_02.pdf.

---

[56] Generally, a release of crude oil to land would not necessarily result in groundwater contamination. In addition to the depth from the land surface to groundwater and the characteristics of the environment into which the crude oil is released (e.g., characteristics of the underlying soils), the potential for crude oil to reach groundwater would depend on factors such as the volume of the spill, the duration of the release, and the viscosity and density of the crude oil.

Impact on U.S. Energy Security

In its Presidential Permit application, TransCanada asserts that constructing the proposed Keystone XL pipeline is in the U.S national interest to maintain adequate crude oil supplies for U.S. refineries. The application argues that the pipeline will allow U.S. refiners to substitute Canadian supply for other foreign crude supply and to obtain direct pipeline access to secure and growing Canadian crude output. In particular, the application asserts that the pipeline would allow the United States to decrease its dependence on foreign crude oil supplies from Mexico and Venezuela, the two largest oil importers into the U.S. Gulf Coast.[57] Consistent with this argument, H.R. 3900 would seek to ensure that any crude oil and bitumen transported by the Keystone XL pipeline, or any resulting refined products, would have to remain in U.S. markets subject to a Presidential waiver allowing foreign export.[58] Depending upon the circumstances, however, such restrictions could raise concerns with respect to international trade agreements, among other considerations.

Energy security arguments have taken on additional weight in light of the recent geopolitical tensions in the Middle East and North Africa. However, it is worth noting that even if Keystone XL is built, prices for the crude oil it carries as well as for domestically produced oil from elsewhere will continue to be affected by international events. The oil market is globally integrated and events in major producer and consumer countries can affect prices everywhere.[59] For example, the disruption of Libyan supply in early 2011 contributed to higher crude oil prices in the United States, even though the United States imported almost no oil from Libya before the unrest broke out.[60]

Canadian Oil Imports in the Overall U.S. Supply Context[61]

Gross U.S. imports of crude oil and petroleum products averaged 11.4 million bpd (Mbpd) in 2011.[62] U.S. oil exports averaged 2.9 Mbpd (almost entirely petroleum products), leaving net imports at 8.4 Mbpd.[63] U.S. net imports have fallen by 4.1 Mbpd or 33% since they peaked in 2005 as a result of lower total oil consumption and higher domestic production. Some of this decline could be mitigated in the near term as oil demand recovers from the recession. However,

---

[57] TransCanada Keystone Pipeline, L.P., September 19, 2008, pp. 6-8.

[58] On February 7, 2012, the House Energy and Committee rejected an amendment to H.R. 3548 offered by Representative Edward Markey containing similar export restrictions.

[59] This is the case unless the oil is stranded due to transport bottlenecks. Ironically, the bottleneck for crude oil flowing south from the Midwest to the Gulf Coast—which Keystone XL would help alleviate—helped insulate Midwestern crude oil prices from the impacts of unrest in the Middle East and North Africa. However, as is discussed below, this may have benefited Midwestern refiners but probably did not significantly reduce costs for U.S. consumers.

[60] For more about this, see CRS Report R41683, *Middle East and North Africa Unrest: Implications for Oil and Natural Gas Markets*, by Michael Ratner and Neelesh Nerurkar.

[61] For a primer on the oil market, see CRS Video Brief *Introduction to the Oil Market*, at http://www.crs.gov/analysis/Pages/WVB00002.aspx.

[62] All data in this section are from the U.S. Energy Information Administration's (EIA's) *Petroleum & Other Liquids* (http://www.eia.gov/petroleum/data.cfm), *International Energy Statistics* (http://tonto.eia.doe.gov/cfapps/ipdbproject/IEDIndex3.cfm), and the *Short Term Energy Outlook* (http://www.eia.gov/forecasts/steo/).

[63] For context, the United States consumed 18.8 Mbpd in 2011, more than 20% of the world's oil market.

Net imports are gross or total imports less total exports. This section will focus on gross imports, though it should be noted that among U.S. petroleum exports about 0.2 Mbpd of petroleum products go to Canada and 0.4 Mbpd to Mexico.

---

there is increasing sentiment among forecasters that U.S. oil imports have passed their high water mark already and may remain relatively flat or fall in the foreseeable future.[64]

Among the largest sources of U.S. gross oil imports are Canada (2.7 Mbpd), the Persian Gulf (1.9 Mbpd), Mexico (1.2 Mbpd), and Venezuela (0.9 Mbpd). Imports from the latter two sources have decreased in recent years in part due to lower need for imports described above and in part due to developments in those countries. Mexican production has been falling since 2004 because new oil developments have not been able to offset depletion at Mexico's giant Cantarell field. Imports from Venezuela, another key source of U.S. imports, have also fallen. Venezuelan production never fully recovered after a strike at its national oil company, *Petróleos de Venezuela*, in 2002-2003. Venezuelan production today is nearly 1 Mbpd less than that achieved in 2001. In recent years, Venezuela has also been trying to diversify business away from the United States, for example, by increasing exports to China.[65]

Meanwhile, Canadian production and exports to the United States have increased, primarily due to growing output from the oil sands in western Canada. Energy markets in the United States and Canada are well integrated by pipeline infrastructure; nearly all Canadian energy exports go to the United States.[66] Canadian oil production has increased about 0.2 Mbpd since 2005 and exports to the United States have increased by 0.5 Mbpd (**see Figure 3**).[67] Some expect Canadian oil production to grow by nearly 2 Mbpd by 2025 due to increased output from the oil sands.[68]

---

[64] For more analysis, see CRS Report R41765, *U.S. Oil Imports: Context and Considerations*, by Neelesh Nerurkar.

[65] U.S. Energy Information Administration, "Country Analysis Brief: Venezuela," February 2010, http://www.eia.doe.gov/emeu/cabs/Venezuela/Oil html.

[66] For further analysis of U.S.-Canada energy trade, see CRS Report R41875, *The U.S.-Canada Energy Relationship: Joined at the Well*, by Paul W. Parfomak and Michael Ratner.

[67] As in the United States, Canadian consumption fell due to economic downturn. This allowed the increment in exports to be higher than the increment in production.

[68] Canadian Association of Petroleum Producers (CAPP), *Crude Oil: Forecast, Markets, and Pipelines*, June 2011, p. 2, http://www.capp.ca/forecast/Pages/default.aspx.

Figure 3. Gross U.S. Oil Imports by Major Sources

Average annual imports in Mbpd

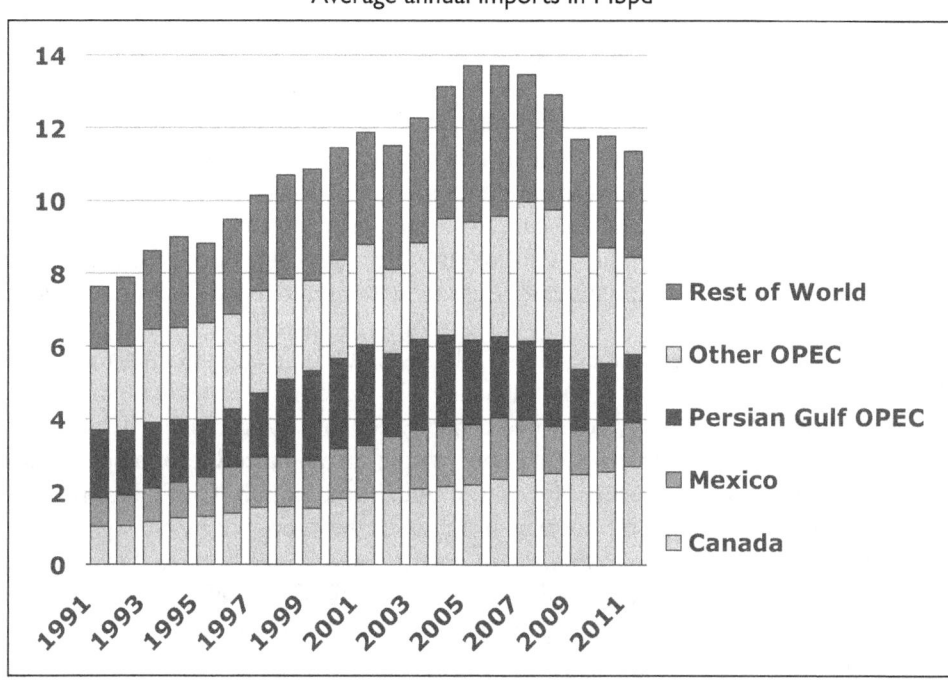

Source: U.S. Energy Information Administration, *Petroleum & Other Liquids: U.S. Imports by Country of Origin*, March 19, 2012. http://www.eia.gov/petroleum/data.cfm#imports.

Oil Sands, Keystone XL, and the U.S. Oil Market

Oil sands (also referred to as tar sands) are a mixture of clay, sand, water, and heavy black viscous oil known as bitumen. Oil sands require more processing than conventional crude oil. Oil sands are processed to extract the bitumen, which can then be sent to refineries in one of two forms. Bitumen can be upgraded into "syncrude," a light crude that is suitable for pipeline transport and is relatively easy to refine. Alternatively, bitumen can be blended with lighter hydrocarbons to form a heavy crude (diluted bitumen or "dilbit") that can be transported by pipeline. The bulk of oil sands supply growth is expected to be in the form of the latter.[69]

Most oil sands imports into the United States currently go to the Midwest, where refineries have been investing in complex refining capacity to process growing volumes of heavy Canadian crude.[70] The U.S. Gulf Coast region already has a large amount of complex refining capacity and is well suited for processing Canadian heavy crude oil. Gulf Coast refiners currently process heavy crudes from Venezuela, Mexico, and elsewhere. Complex refineries in the Gulf Coast may be best equipped to handle a large increase of heavy oil sands crude, though they may still need to adjust processes and make new capital investments in equipment to accommodate particular crudes' characteristics,[71] especially if the new Canadian crudes will be used in large amounts.[72]

---

[69] CAPP, 2011, p. 7.

[70] CAPP, 2011, p. 13. According to CAPP, refineries adding capacity to process more heavy oil in the Midwest include those in Roxana, IL; Whiting, IN; and Detroit, MI.

[71] Baker Hughes, *Planning Ahead for Effective Canadian Crude Processing*, Baker Petrolite White Paper, 2010, http://www.bakerhughes.com/assets/media/whitepapers/4c2a3c8ffa7e1c3c7400001d/file/28271-
(continued...)

There are 15 refineries within Keystone XL's proposed delivery area in Texas that currently process heavy crude oil similar in composition to the oil that Keystone XL pipeline would carry.[73]

Oil production from the oil sands is increasing, as is production from the Bakken and other areas of the U.S. Midwest.[74] Transport options to carry crude from the Midwest to the Gulf Coast are limited. (In the past, crude oil had been shipped up from the Gulf Coast to Midwestern refineries). The resulting abundance of crude oil in the Midwest has driven down crude oil prices in that region relative to Gulf Coast and international crude markets. Midwestern refiners benefit from the lower cost of crude, but it does not translate to substantially lower consumer prices for gasoline or other products in the region. The Midwest still brings in refined products from the Gulf Coast, which keeps refined products prices in line with national and international levels.[75]

Oil sands producers are interested in Keystone XL because it would expand their market reach into the Gulf Coast. The Gulf Coast region holds half of U.S. refining capacity, including a substantial amount of technologically advanced capacity capable of processing heavy sour crudes in large volumes. Reaching a larger market and one with more advanced refining capacity could increase the price these producers receive for their crude. For their part, Gulf Coast refiners are interested in the Keystone XL pipeline because it increases the supply of heavy sour crude in the Gulf region, potentially bringing down their input costs relative to the options they currently have available. Canadian Natural Resources Limited, an oil sands producer, and Valero Energy Corporation, a large U.S. refiner, are among those that contracted for shipping capacity on the Keystone XL pipeline.

With expanded pipeline capacity extending to the U.S. Gulf Coast, Canadian oil sands crude may compete with other heavy crudes such as those from Mexico, Venezuela, and elsewhere.[76] It is difficult to predict precisely how this competition will play out, but it may take place through shifting discounts or premiums on crude oils from various sources.[77] It may be possible for Canadian oil supplies to effectively "push out" waterborne shipments from other countries, although this depends on a wide range of market conditions. Waterborne crudes may more easily go to other destinations than Canadian crudes, though like Canadian crudes they can be tied to specialized refining capacity, as is true for Venezuelan heavy crudes.

There is concern that increased supply of crude to the Gulf Coast may result in larger petroleum product exports rather than contributing to lower domestic fuel cost. Although the United States is a net importer of oil and petroleum products, it does export some petroleum products. U.S.

(...continued)

canadian_crudeoil_update_whitepaper_06-10.pdf.pdf&fs=1497549.

[72] For a description of which units refineries may need to add (or have added) to be able to process more Canadian oil sands supply, see Praveen Gunaseelan and Christopher Buehler, "Changing US Crude Imports Are Driving Refinery Upgrades," *Oil and Gas Journal*, August 10, 2009.

[73] U.S. Department of State, April 15, 2011. p. 1-4.

[74] See increased U.S. crude oil production in the Midwest under the PADD2 heading at the following source: Energy Information Administration, U.S. Department of Energy, *Crude Oil Production (by PADD)*, Petroleum & Other Liquids, http://www.eia.gov/dnav/pet/pet_crd_crpdn_adc_mbblpd_a htm.

[75] Adjusted for transport costs and other regional differences.

[76] Center for Energy Economics and Bureau of Economic Geology, *Overview of the Alberta Oil Sands*, University of Texas at Austin, 2006, p. 16, http://www.beg.utexas.edu/energyecon/documents/overview_of_alberta_oil_sands.pdf.

[77] For more about the U.S. refining system, see CRS Report R41478, *The U.S. Oil Refining Industry: Background in Changing Markets and Fuel Policies*, by Anthony Andrews, Robert Pirog, and Molly F. Sherlock.

petroleum product exports rose when domestic demand declined in the wake of the recession while foreign demand for certain fuels, such as diesel, remained relatively robust. Issues around potential export of Canadian crude oil carried on Keystone XL or export of products made from that crude oil are addressed in CRS Report R42465, *U.S. Oil Imports and Exports*, by Neelesh Nerurkar.

If Keystone XL secures growing oil sands output for the United States, it could push out seaborne crudes from elsewhere, regardless of where the product is ultimately sold. If the absence of the pipeline encourages Canadian oil sands producers and pipeline companies to find an alternate export route through the Canadian West Coast, Canadian supplies may displace heavy oil supplies in other markets and potentially allow relatively more overseas imports coming into the Gulf Coast. This possibility is discussed further below.

It should be noted that Keystone XL aims to alleviate two potential bottlenecks in the pipeline transportation system: Between Western Canada and the United States, and between the U.S. Midwest and the Gulf Coast. Existing pipelines between Canada and the United States have spare capacity to carry rising Canadian production for the time being. According to some estimates, additional capacity, such as Keystone XL, may not be needed until 2019.[78] The latter bottleneck, between the Midwest and the Gulf Coast, is already at capacity and, as described above, has resulted in a discount for crude oil in the Midwest (though not for petroleum products). The Gulf Coast Pipeline Project, the lower leg of originally proposed Keystone XL pipeline, would address this second bottleneck and help alleviate the discount for Midwestern crudes.

Other Pipeline Projects

Apart from Keystone XL, several other pipeline proposals could help carry growing Canadian crude oil supplies to the U.S. Gulf Coast. On October 16, 2011, Enbridge announced it would purchase ConocoPhillips' share of the Seaway pipeline and reverse its direction to bring crude oil from the Midwest to the Gulf Coast. ConocoPhillips had kept the pipeline running northward to serve its refinery in Ponca City, OK. However, the glut of oil in the Midwest had resulted in the pipeline running at low volumes. Nonetheless, ConocoPhillips had been uninterested in reversing the pipeline. ConocoPhillips, which is spinning off its refining business,[79] sold its share of Seaway to Enbridge. Enbridge and Seaway shareholder Enterprise Products Partners L.P. are reversing the direction of crude oil flows on the Seaway pipeline to enable it to transport oil from Cushing, OK, to the U.S. Gulf Coast. The pipeline is expected to start running southward at an initial capacity of 150,000 bpd starting in May 2012, with capacity expected to increase to 400,000 bpd in 2013. The reversal is expected to reduce the glut of crude oil in the Midwest and reconnect Midwestern crude prices to global prices (driving the U.S. Benchmark West Texas Intermediate crude higher).[80]

Prior to the Seaway sale, Enbridge had reported significant commitments for two new pipeline projects: Flanagan South, which would carry oil from Illinois to Oklahoma, and Wrangler, which

---

[78] Testimony of Jim Burkhard, U.S. Congress, Senate Committee on Energy and Natural Resources, *US and Global Energy Outlook for 2012*, 112th Cong., 2nd sess., January 31, 2012.

[79] ConocoPhillips, "ConocoPhillips Pursuing Plan to Separate into Two Stand-Alone, Publicly Traded Companies," press release, July 14, 2011, http://www.conocophillips.com/EN/newsroom/news_releases/2011news/Pages/07-14-2011.aspx.

[80] Jenny Gross, "NYMEX Oil Gets Boost From Pipeline Reversal," *Wall Street Journal*, April 22, 2012.

would carry oil from Oklahoma to Texas.[81] According to Enbridge, the project would duplicate existing routes and would not cross an international border, so it would not require a Presidential Permit. Enbridge already has cross border pipeline capacity connecting Alberta to Illinois. However, according to press reports, Wrangler has been canceled in light of the Seaway purchase and reversal.[82] Enbridge is moving forward with the Flanagan South project, which will have an initial capacity of about 600,000 bpd and run alongside Enbridge's existing Spearhead pipeline (see **Figure 4**).[83] Like Keystone XL, Flanagan South and a southbound Seaway may facilitate increased flow of Canadian crude to the U.S. Gulf Coast.

Figure 4. Proposed Enbridge Flanagan South Pipeline Route

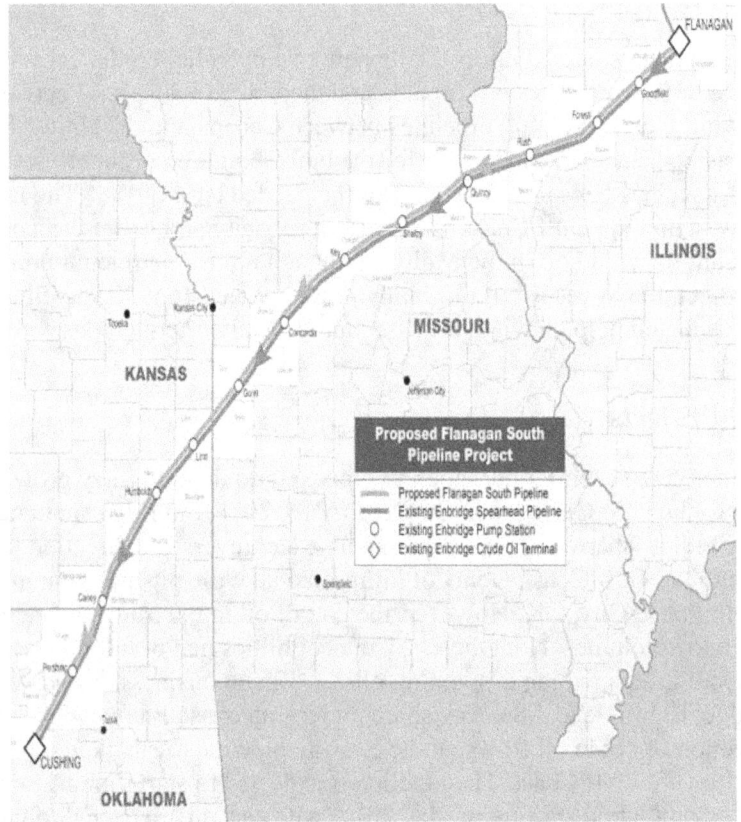

Source: Enbridge, "Flanagan South Project Fact Sheet," April 1, 2012, http://www.enbridge.com/ FlanaganSouthPipeline.aspx.

Canadian Oil to Alternative Markets

There are proposals to increase the capacity for oil from Alberta to reach the Canadian east and west coast. Currently, nearly all of Canada's oil exports go to the United States, mostly through north-south pipelines. Only one major oil pipeline extends from Alberta to Canada's west coast:

---

[81] Bradley Olson , "Enbridge Pursuing Alternative to Transcanada's Keystone XL," *Bloomberg*, November 9, 2011.

[82] Ben Lefebvre, "Enterprise Products Cancels Wrangler Pipeline," Dow Jones Newswires, November 16, 2011.

[83] Enbridge, "Flanagan South Project Fact Sheet," April 1, 2012, http://www.enbridge.com/ FlanaganSouthPipeline.aspx.

the Trans Mountain Pipeline, which is owned by Houston-based Kinder Morgan and has a capacity of 300,000 bpd. Some of the oil from the Trans Mountain Pipeline is loaded onto tankers and shipped from Vancouver. Nearly all of the quantities shipped by sea go to the United States, though a small amount goes to China and other Asian countries.[84] Proposals for additional East and Westbound capacity include:

- Kinder Morgan has plans to expand the Trans Mountain Pipeline to 850,000 bpd by 2017, more than doubling its existing capacity, and expanding west coast shipping facilities.[85] The expansion has received the necessary commitments from parties interested in shipping additional crude volumes. Some shippers are interested in using the additional capacity to export more Canadian crude oil to Asia. Kinder Morgan still needs regulatory approvals from Canadian authorities and is working to gain the support of stake holders.[86] There is some opposition to the project, including from groups concerned about additional tanker traffic near Vancouver and potential oil spill risks.[87]

- Enbridge has proposed a new pipeline: the Northern Gateway project would have a 525,000 bpd capacity to send oil from Edmonton to Kimat, British Columbia.[88] However, Northern Gateway faces opposition from groups including some First Nations communities and environmental groups.[89]

- Several projects are considering moving oil east rather than to the west coast. According to reports, TransCanada is considering a pipeline project sending oil east from Alberta to Quebec and New Brunswick which could also carry crude bound for export.[90] Enbridge is also interested in expanding eastbound capacity by reversing its Line 9 Pipeline.[91] Some suggest this could potentially lead to oil sands crude traveling east, through Montreal and then through another pipeline to Portland, Maine, from which point it could be exported.[92] As with other pipeline projects, these also face opposition from environmental groups concerned about oil spill risks and/or generally opposed to oil sands development.

These projects reflect anticipated growth of western Canadian oil production and an interest by Canadian oil producers to diversify their available markets beyond U.S. customers, including to

---

[84] According to the Global Trade Atlas, about 0.5% of Canadian crude exports went to China in 2011 (accessed April 25, 2012).

[85] Christopher Smith, "KMEP Advances Trans Moutain Crude Pipeline Expansion," *Oil & Gas Journal*, April 6, 2012.

[86] David Ebner and Justine Hunter, "U.S. Company Plans Billion-Dollar Expansion of Trans Mountain Pipeline," *The Global and Mail*, April 13, 2012.

[87] Jeff Lee, "Vancouver Council, Park Board to Formally Oppose Kinder Morgan Pipeline Expansion," *Vancover Sun*, April 24, 2012.

[88] Enbridge, "Northern Gateway at a Glance," press release, 2011, http://www northerngateway.ca/project-info/ northern-gateway-at-a-glance. The project would also include a pipeline to allow the import of 193,000 bpd of condensate, a light hydrocarbon that can be blended with bitumen to allow pipeline transport.

[89] "Enbridge Pipeline and Tanker Opposition Mounts as Risks Multiply," *Marketwire*, March 13, 2012.

[90] Nathan Vanderklippe and Shawn McCarthy, "TransCanada Looks East as Gateway Pipeline Gets Bogged Down," *The Globae and Mail*, March 22, 2012.

[91] "Enbridge Pipelines Inc. - Line 9 Reversal Phase I Project (OH-005-2011)," (Project Application), National Energy Board (Government of Canada), http://www neb-one.gc.ca/clf-nsi/rthnb/pplctnsbfrthnb/nbrdgln9phs1/nbrdgln9phs1-eng html.

[92] Matt Dodge, "Court Decision Affects South Portland-Montreal Pipeline," *Maine Biz*, April 3, 2012.

reach rapidly growing Asian oil demand. Proposals have received criticism from environmentalists. Because it would require construction of a completely new pipeline, Northern Gateway in particular has been criticized by some environmental and First Nations groups.[93]

Canadian interests assert that Canadian oil sales to Asian markets, where oil demand is growing rapidly, are more likely if greater shipments to the United States are not possible.[94] A study commissioned by the U.S. Department of Energy suggested that:

> if pipeline projects to the BC [British Columbia] coast are built, they are likely to be utilized. This is because of the relatively short marine distances to major northeast Asia markets, future expected growth there in refining capacity and increasing ownership interests by Chinese companies especially in oil sands production. Such increased capacity would alter global crude trade patterns. Western Canadian Sedimentary Basin (WCSB) crudes would be "lost" from the USA, going instead to Asia. There they would displace the world's balancing crude oils, Middle Eastern and African predominantly OPEC grades, which would in turn move to the USA. The net effect would be substantially higher U.S. dependency on crude oils from those sources versus scenarios where capacity to move WCSB crudes to Asia was limited.[95]

Economic Impact of the Pipeline

In addition to supply diversity arguments, some Keystone XL pipeline proponents support the project based on economic benefits associated with expanding U.S. pipeline infrastructure. A recent study by the Energy Policy Research Foundation, for example, concludes that "the Keystone expansion would provide net economic benefits from improved efficiencies in both the transportation and processing of crude oil of $100 million-$600 million annually, in addition to an immediate boost in construction employment."[96] A 2009 report from the Canadian Energy Research Institute (CERI) commissioned by the American Petroleum Institute similarly concludes that

> As investment and production in oil sands ramps up in Canada, the pace of economic activity quickens and demand for US goods and services increase rapidly, resulting in an estimated 343 thousand new US jobs between 2011 and 2015. Demand for U.S. goods and services continues to climb throughout the period, adding an estimated $34 billion to US GDP in 2015, $40.4 billion in 2020, and $42.2 billion in 2025.[97]

These CERI estimates apply to the entire oil sands industry, however, not only the Keystone XL project, and they are derived from a proprietary economic analysis which has not been subject to external review. Some stakeholders point to State Department and other studies reporting much

---

[93] Derrick Penner, "Opposition to Enbridge Northern Gateway pipeline grows," *Vancouver Sun*, December 2, 2010.

[94] Edward Welsch, "TransCanada: Oil Sands Exports Will Go to Asia if Blocked in U.S.," Dow Jones Newswires, June 30, 2010.

[95] EnSys Energy & Systems, Inc., *Keystone XL Assessment: Final Report*, Prepared for the U.S. Department of Energy, Office of Policy & International Affairs, December 23, 2010, p. 118.

[96] Energy Policy Research Foundation, Inc., The Value of the Canadian Oil Sands (....to the United States): An Assessment of the Keystone Proposal to Expand Oil Sands Shipments to Gulf Coast Refiners, Washington, DC, November 29, 2010, p. 2, http://www.eprinc.org/pdf/oilsandsvalue.pdf.

[97] Canadian Energy Research Institute, *The Impacts of Canadian Oil Sands Development on the United States' Economy, Final Report*, Calgary, Alberta, October 2009, p. vii.

---

lower anticipated economic benefits.[98] Consequently, it is difficult to determine what specific economic and employment impacts may ultimately be attributable to the Keystone XL pipeline. Nonetheless, given the physical scale of the project, it could be expected to increase employment and investment at least during construction.

Lifecycle Greenhouse Gas Emissions

Oil production from oil sands is controversial because it has significant environmental impacts, including emissions of greenhouse gases during extraction and processing, disturbance of mined land, and impacts on wildlife and water quality.[99] Because bitumen in oil sands cannot be pumped from a conventional well, it must be mined, usually using strip mining or open pit techniques, or the oil can be extracted with underground heating methods.[100] Large amounts of water and natural gas are also required (for heating) during the extraction process.[101] The magnitude of the environmental impacts of oil sands production, in absolute terms and compared to conventional oil production, has been the subject of numerous, and sometimes conflicting, studies and policy papers.[102] Some stakeholders who object to oil sands projects oppose the Keystone XL pipeline because it expands access to new markets for the oil produced by those projects, thereby encouraging what they consider to be further environmentally destructive oil sands development. As discussed earlier, however, if oil sands production can be diverted to other markets (e.g., Asia), preventing the Keystone XL project may not necessarily limit oil sands development.[103]

Some stakeholders object to the Keystone XL pipeline because it would increase U.S. supplies of oil, and thereby perpetuate the nation's dependence on imported fossil fuels and increase carbon emissions from the transportation sector.[104] Acknowledging this concern, in a public forum on October 20, 2010, Secretary of State Clinton reportedly remarked that "we're either going to be dependent on dirty oil from the [Persian] Gulf or dirty oil from Canada ... until we can get our act together as a country and figure out that clean, renewable energy is in both our economic interests and the interests of our planet."[105] Critics of the State Department's draft and supplemental draft EIS assert that the environmental review overlooks the pipeline project's overall impact on greenhouse gas emissions, for example, from the extraction and refining processes. To address those potential emissions, EPA recommended that the final EIS include discussion of mitigation

---

[98] See, for example, Cornell University Global Labor Institute, *Pipe Dreams? Jobs Gained, Jobs Lost by the Construction of Keystone XL*, September 28, 2011; National Wildlife Federation, "TransCanada Exaggerating Jobs Claims for Keystone XL," November 9, 2010, http://www.dirtyoilsands.org/files/Keystone_XL_Jobs_11-09-10.pdf.

[99] For more analysis of oil sands and their environmental impacts, see CRS Report RL34258, *North American Oil Sands: History of Development, Prospects for the Future*, by Marc Humphries.

[100] U.S. Bureau of Land Management, "About Tar Sands," web page, January 11, 2011, http://ostseis.anl.gov/guide/tarsands/index.cfm.

[101] Cecilia Jamasmie, "The Challenges and Potential of Canada's Oil Sands," *Mining*, September-October 2010, pp. 7-8.

[102] For an example of contrasting views, see IHS CERA Inc., *Oil Sands, Greenhouse Gases, and US Oil Supply, Getting the Numbers Right*, 2010; and Natural Resources Defense Council, "Setting the Record Straight: Lifecycle Emissions of Tar Sands," November 2010.

[103] For more analysis of oil sands, including the environmental effects of its extraction, see CRS Report RL34258, *North American Oil Sands: History of Development, Prospects for the Future*, by Marc Humphries.

[104] See, for example: Natural Resources Defense Council, *Tar Sands Invasion: How Dirty and Expensive Oil from Canada Threatens America's New Energy Economy*, May 2010.

[105] See Secretary of State Hillary Clinton's "Remarks on Innovation and American Leadership to the Commonwealth Club," San Francisco, CA, October 15, 2010, available at http://www.state.gov/secretary/rm/2010/10/149542 htm.

---

approaches for greenhouse gas emissions from extraction activities that are either currently used or could be employed to help lower lifecycle greenhouse gas emissions.[106] However, others have argued that whether the Keystone XL Pipeline is constructed would have little bearing on greenhouse gas emissions as there are likely to be other export routes available for Canadian oil sands crude, and therefore, the same crude oils would still be transported and refined, albeit in different locations.[107]

Land Use and Oil Spill Impacts

For the pipeline project represented in the August 2011 final EIS, approximately 95% of the land affected by pipeline construction and operation was privately owned, with the remaining 5% almost equally state and federal land. Private land uses were primarily agricultural—farmers and cattle ranchers.

The pipeline's construction and continued operation would involve a 50-foot-wide permanent right-of-way along the length of the pipeline. Keystone agreed to compensate landowners for losses on a case-by-case basis. However, a concern among landowners and communities along the route is the potential for their land or water (used for drinking, irrigation, or recreation) to be contaminated by an accidental release (spill) of oil. That concern is heightened in areas where the pipeline will be located near or would cross water or is in a remote location.

A primary environmental concern of any oil pipeline is the risk of a spill. In estimating the possible impacts of an oil spill, location is generally considered the most important factor—particularly the potential for the spill to reach surface or groundwater. For example, the potential impacts of a spill to water is highlighted in the Keystone XL final EIS, as follows:

> The greatest concern would be a spill in environmentally sensitive areas, such as wetlands, flowing streams and rivers, shallow groundwater areas, areas near water intakes for drinking water or for commercial/industrial uses, and areas with populations of sensitive wildlife or plant species.[108]

A release of oil on land would not necessarily result in surface or groundwater contamination. The potential for a spill to reach water would depend on factors such its proximity to a water source (e.g., on or near a creek or stream or located on land where the groundwater table is close to the surface) and the characteristics of the environment into which the crude oil is released (e.g., porous underlying soils), and the volume of the spill, the duration of the release, and the viscosity and density of the crude oil.

The size of potential spills and the type of oil that would likely be released from the Keystone XL pipeline have been issues of concern to opponents of the project. In its July 16, 2010, comments on the draft EIS for the Keystone XL pipeline, EPA expressed particular concern over the potential adverse impacts to surface and ground water from pipeline leaks or spills. That concern

---

[106] See EPA's July 16, 2010, letter to the State Department rating the supplemental EIS for the Keystone XL pipeline project, available at http://yosemite.epa.gov/oeca/webeis nsf/%28PDFView%29/20100126/$file/20100126.PDF. Discussion of the analysis of GHG emissions is included on pp. 3-4.

[107] EnSys Energy & Systems 2010, p. 116.

[108] U.S. Department of State, *Final Environmental Impact Statement for the Proposed Keystone XL Project*, August 2011, p. ES-9.

stemmed from two areas—the toxicity of chemical diluents that may be used to allow bitumen to be transported by pipeline and the lack of risk assessment for potential "serious or significant spills," including an evaluation of spill response procedures in the wake of such a spill.

Concerns reflected in EPA's letter were realized 10 days later when the Enbridge Energy Partners' Alberta Pipeline ruptured near Marshall, MI. The resulting spill released dilbit crude into a tributary creek of the Kalamazoo River and traveled approximately 40 miles downstream in the Kalamazoo River. Initially estimated by Enbridge as a release of approximately 800,000 gallons of crude, EPA subsequently estimated that over 1.1 million gallons were released. The spill resulted in over 220 areas of moderate-to-heavy contamination, including over 200 acres of submerged oil on the river bottom and over 300 solidified oil deposits.[109] Enbridge estimates that cleanup will cost approximately $700 million.

The Enbridge spill highlighted several issues of concern among environmental groups and communities along the pipeline route—in particular, the nature of the dilbit crude likely carried by the Keystone XL pipeline. The dilbit crude in the Enbridge spill had been diluted with benzene and other hazardous constituents. Following the spill, high levels of benzene in the air prompted the issuance of voluntary evacuation of residents in the area. Concern over the presence of similarly toxic constituents, particularly the degree to which the level of toxic constituents may be unknown at the time of a release, has been an ongoing concern among environmental and community groups.

The Enbridge spill was considered a "very large spill" and not necessarily one that would likely occur along the Keystone XL pipeline route. However, in its first year of operation, TransCanada's Keystone pipeline experienced 14 spills. Although mostly minor spills, one spill at the Ludden, ND, pump station resulted in the release of 21,000 gallons of oil. Like the Enbridge release, that release was first reported by local citizens, not as a result of the Keystone's release detection equipment. These incidents have made pipeline opponents concerned that, absent a witness to a spill, a leak in a remote area could potentially go undetected for a long period.

Also as illustrated in the aftermath of the Enbridge spill, cleanup of bitumen crude presents certain challenges. Dilbit is a relatively heavy crude oil mixture compared to other crude oils. In general, heavier oils are more persistent and present greater technical challenges in removal after a spill compared to lighter oils. Almost two years after the Enbridge spill, cleanup efforts continue. Since the spill, public access to 39 miles of the river system was banned to protect public health and safety. The first three-mile segment of river reopened to the public on April 27, 2012. Elements of the cleanup are expected to last until 2015.

Regardless of design, construction, and safety measures, the Keystone XL pipeline will likely have some number of spills over the course of its operating life. The unique oil spill response efforts necessary for dilbit crude make an accurate assessment of potential oil spill risk particularly relevant when addressing concerns expressed by opponents to the Keystone XL pipeline. The need for more conclusive analysis of potential risks associated with the transport of dilbit crude was addressed, in part, in the Pipeline Safety, Regulatory Certainty, and Job Creation Act of 2011 (P.L. 112-90, enacted January 16, 2012). In particular, under Section 16, "Study of transportation of diluted bitumen," the Secretary of Transportation is required to conduct an

---

[109] For more information see EPA's regarding the response to the Enbridge oil spill at http://www.epa.gov/enbridgespill/.

analysis to determine whether there is any increased risk of a release for pipeline facilities transporting diluted bitumen. In response to that directive, the PHMSA contracted with the National Academy of Sciences to conduct a full and independent study of this topic.

Appendix A. Presidential Permitting Authority[110]

The executive branch has exercised permitting authority over the construction and operation of "pipelines, conveyor belts, and similar facilities for the exportation or importation of petroleum, petroleum products" and other products at least since the promulgation of Executive Order 11423 in 1968.[111] Executive Order 13337 amended this authority and the procedures associated with the review, but did not substantially alter the exercise of authority or the delegation to the Secretary of State in E.O. 11423.[112] However, the source of the executive branch's permitting authority is not entirely clear from the text of these Executive Orders. Generally, powers exercised by the executive branch are authorized by legislation or are inherent presidential powers based in the Constitution. E.O. 11423 makes no mention of any authority, and E.O. 13337 refers only to the "Constitution and the Laws of the United States of America, including Section 301 of title 3, United States Code."[113] Section 301 simply provides that the President is empowered to delegate authority to the head of any department or agency of the executive branch.

The legitimacy of this permitting authority has been addressed by federal courts. In *Sisseton v. United States Department of State*, the plaintiff Tribes filed suit and asked the court to suspend or revoke the Presidential Permit issued under E.O. 13337 for the TransCanada Keystone Pipeline.[114] The U.S. District Court for the District of South Dakota found that the plaintiffs lacked standing because they would be unable to prove their injury could be redressed by a favorable decision.[115] The court determined that even if the plaintiff's injury could be redressed, "the President would be free to disregard the court's judgment," as the case concerned the President's "inherent Constitutional authority to conduct foreign policy," as opposed to statutory authority granted to the President by Congress.[116]

The court further found that even if the Tribes had standing, the issuance of the Presidential Permit was a presidential action, not an agency action subject to judicial review under the Administrative Procedure Act (APA).[117] The court stated that the authority to regulate the cross-border pipeline lies with either Congress or the President.[118] The court found that "Congress has failed to create a federal regulatory scheme for the construction of oil pipelines, and has delegated this authority to the states. Therefore, the President has the sole authority to allow oil pipeline border crossings under his inherent constitutional authority to conduct foreign affairs."[119] The

---

[110] For a more expansive treatment of this topic, see CRS Report R42124, *Proposed Keystone XL Pipeline: Legal Issues*, by Adam Vann et al.

[111] *Providing for the performance of certain functions heretofore performed by the President with respect to certain facilities constructed and maintained on the borders of the United States*, 33 *Federal Register* 11741, August 16, 1968.

[112] *Issuance of Permits With Respect to Certain Energy-Related Facilities and Land Transportation Crossings on the International Boundaries of the United States*, 69 *Federal Register* 25299, May 5, 2004.

[113] Ibid.

[114] 659 F. Supp. 2d 1071, 1078 (D. S.D. 2009).

[115] Ibid. at 1078.

[116] Ibid. at 1078, 1078 n.5.

[117] See ibid. at 1080-81.

[118] Ibid. at 1081.

[119] Ibid.

President could delegate his permitting authority to the U.S. Department of State, but delegation did not transform the permit's issuance into an agency action reviewable under the APA.[120]

In *Sierra Club v. Clinton*,[121] the plaintiff Sierra Club challenged the Secretary of State's decision to issue a Presidential Permit authorizing the Alberta Clipper pipeline. Among the plaintiff's claims was an allegation that issuance of the permit was unconstitutional because the President had no authority to issue the permits referenced in E.O. 13337 (in this case, for the importation of crude oil from Canada via pipeline).[122] The defendant responded that the authority to issue Presidential Permits for these border-crossing facilities "does not derive from a delegation of congressional authority ... but rather from the President's constitutional authority over foreign affairs and his authority as Commander in Chief."[123] The U.S. District Court for the District of Minnesota agreed, noting that the defendant's assertion regarding the source of the President's authority has been "well recognized" in a series of Attorney General opinions, as well as a 2009 judicial opinion.[124] The court also noted that these permits had been issued many times before and that "Congress has not attempted to exercise any exclusive authority over the permitting process. Congress's inaction suggests that Congress has accepted the authority of the President to issue cross-border permits."[125] Based on the historical recognition of the President's authority to issue these permits and Congress's implied approval through inaction, the court found the Presidential Permit requirement for border facilities constitutional.

---

[120] Ibid. at 1082.

[121] 689 F.Supp.2d 1147 (D. Minn. 2010).

[122] Ibid. at 1162.

[123] Ibid.

[124] Ibid. at 1163 (citing 38 U.S. Atty Gen. 162 (1935); 30 U.S. Op. Atty. Gen. 217 (1913); 24 U.S. Op. Atty. Gen. 100; and Natural Resources Defense Council (NRDC) v. U.S. Department of State, 658 F.Supp.2d 105, 109 (D.D.C. 2009)). The court in *NRDC* held that the State Department's issuance of a presidential permit under Executive Order 13337 was not subject to judicial review under the Administrative Procedure Act for abuse of discretion because "the issuance of presidential permits is ultimately a presidential action." 658 F. Supp. 2d at 109, 111-12. The court said that to allow judicial review of such decisions would raise separation of powers concerns. Ibid. at 111.

[125] Ibid.; see also Youngstown Sheet and Tube Co. v. Sawyer, 343 U.S. 579 (1952) (establishing a three-part test for analyzing the validity of presidential actions in relation to constitutional and congressional authority).

Appendix B. Milestones in the Initial NEPA Process

The NEPA process for TransCanada's 2008 Presidential Permit application for the Keystone XL pipeline project included several significant milestones (summarized in **Table 1**). These events, and resulting documents, will likely have varying degrees of influence over TransCanada's 2012 permit application.

Draft EIS issued

The State Department released its draft EIS for the proposed Keystone XL Pipeline project for public comment on April 16, 2010.[126] The draft EIS identified TransCanada's "preferred alternative" for the project as well as other alternatives considered. On July 16, 2010, EPA rated the draft EIS "Inadequate."[127] EPA found that potentially significant impacts were not evaluated and that the additional information and analysis needed was of such importance that the draft EIS would need to be formally revised and again made available for public review. Additional criticism of the State Department's implementation of the NEPA process followed an October 21, 2010, statement by Secretary Clinton that, while analysis of the project was not complete and a final decision had not been made, the State Department was "inclined to" approve the project.[128] Critics of the project, including some Members of Congress, stated that the Secretary's statement appeared to prejudge its permit approval for the pipeline proposal as a foregone conclusion.[129]

Supplemental Draft EIS Issued

The State Department issued a supplemental draft EIS on April 15, 2011. In addition to addressing issues associated with EPA's inadequacy rating, the supplemental draft EIS addressed comments received from other agencies and the public. On June 6, 2011, EPA sent a letter to the State Department that rated the supplemental draft EIS as having "Insufficient Information" and having "Environmental Objections" to the proposed action.[130] EPA acknowledged that the State Department had "worked diligently" to develop additional information in response to EPA's comments and the large number of other comments on the draft EIS. However, EPA believed that additional analysis needed to be included in the final EIS to fully respond to its earlier comments.

---

[126] Documents submitted for the initial 2008 Presidential Permit application have now been archived by the State Department. Documents related to that original application are available at http://keystonepipeline-xl.state.gov/archive/index htm.

[127] U.S. Environmental Protection Agency's July 16, 2010, letter to the U.S. Department of State commenting on the draft EIS for the Keystone XL project is available at http://yosemite.epa.gov/oeca/webeis.nsf/%28PDFView%29/20100126/$file/20100126.PDF.

[128] See Secretary of State Hillary Clinton, "Remarks on Innovation and American Leadership to the Commonwealth Club," San Francisco, CA, October 15, 2010, available at http://www.state.gov/secretary/rm/2010/10/149542 htm. The statement by Secretary Clinton was actually made in response to a question about the Alberta Clipper pipeline project which received a Presidential Permit from the State Department in 2009; a State Department spokesman later clarified that the Secretary was referring to the Keystone XL pipeline permit approval.

[129] For example, see the October 21, 2010, letter from Senator Mike Johanns to Secretary Clinton expressing his concern that her statement gave the appearance that approval of the pipeline was a foregone conclusion, http://johanns.senate.gov/public/?a=Files.Serve&File_id=8b090aa5-76fe-41ca-a674-ae9e37db8d36.

[130] U.S. Environmental Protection Agency's June 6, 2011, letter to the U.S. Department of State commenting on the supplemental draft EIS for the Keystone XL project is available at http://yosemite.epa.gov/oeca/webeis nsf/%28PDFView%29/20110125/$file/20110125.PDF?OpenElement.

Among other items, EPA recommended that the State Department should do the following: improve the analysis of the potential oil spill risks, including additional analysis of other reasonable alternatives to the proposed pipeline route; provide additional analysis of potential oil spill impacts, health impacts, and environmental justice concerns to communities along the pipeline route and adjacent refineries; and improve its characterization of lifecycle greenhouse gas emissions associated with Canadian oil sands crude.

In its June 6th letter to the State Department, EPA refers to agreements with the State Department that certain deficiencies identified in the supplemental draft EIS would be addressed in the final EIS. Further, in its conclusion, EPA stated that it would carefully review the final EIS to determine if it fully reflects those agreements and if measures to mitigate adverse environmental impacts are fully evaluated.

Final EIS Issued

On August 26, 2011, the State Department issued the final EIS for the proposed Keystone XL Pipeline. Among other elements of the final EIS, it identified various major pipeline route alternatives and an environmental analyses of potential impacts associated with those alternatives.[131]

In October 2011, 14 Members of Congress wrote to the State Department's Office of Inspector General requesting an investigation of the department's handling of the EIS and National Interest Determination for the Keystone XL project.[132] The request was prompted, in part, by press reports suggesting bias or potential conflicts of interest in the State Department's hiring of an outside contractor to perform the EIS and in its communications with the pipeline's developer, TransCanada.[133] On November 4, the Inspector General's Office (IG) announced that, in response to this request, it was initiating a special review "to determine to what extent the Department and all other parties involved complied with Federal laws and regulations relating to the Keystone XL pipeline permit process."[134] On February 9, 2012, the IG released its findings, reporting that the State Department "did not violate its role as an unbiased oversight agency," among other specific findings generally supportive of the department's Keystone XL permit review process.[135]

Public Review and National Interest Determination

Following the release of the Keystone XL project's final EIS, a review period began to determine if the proposed project was in the national interest. As part of the process for the Keystone XL project, the State Department held public meetings in each of the six states through which the

---

[131] Environmental analysis associated with pipeline project alternatives is provided in Volumes 1 and 2 of the final EIS.

[132] U.S. Senator Bernard Sanders, et al., Letter to The Honorable Harold W. Geisel, Office of Inspector General, U.S. Department of State, October 26, 2011.

[133] See. for example, Elisabeth Rosenthal and Dan Frosch, "Pipeline Review Is Faced with Question of Conflict," *New York Times*, October 7, 2011.

[134] Harold W. Geisel, United States Department of State, Office of Inspector General, "Information Memo for Deputy Secretary Burns," November 4, 2011, http://sanders.senate.gov/imo/media/doc/ Special%20Review%20Keystone%20XL%20Pipeline%20Nov%2020112.pdf.

[135] Harold W. Geisel, United States Department of State, Office of Inspector General, *Special Review of the Keystone XL Pipeline Permit Process*, AUD/SI-12-28, February 2012.

---

proposed pipeline would pass and in Washington, DC.[136] The meetings were intended to give members of the public additional opportunity to voice their opinions on issues they thought should be taken into account in determining whether granting or denying the Presidential Permit would be in the national interest.[137] During the review period, the State Department received input from state, local, and tribal officials as well as members of the public.

After the public review period, the State Department issued a statement regarding the public comments and its response to those comments.[138] The State Department stated that it received comments on a wide range of issues, including the Keystone XL project's potential impact on jobs, pipeline safety, health concerns, the societal impact of the project, and oil extraction in Canada. Concern regarding the proposed pipeline route through the Sand Hills area of Nebraska was identified as one of the most common issues raised. Comments regarding that pipeline route were consistent with the environmental impacts identified in the final EIS with regard to the unique combination of characteristics of the Sand Hills region.

To understand the concerns associated with potential environmental impacts of the construction and operation of a pipeline that crosses the Sand Hills (also referred to as the Sandhills), an understanding of the unique size and structure of the region is useful. It is a 19,600 square mile sand dune formation stabilized by native grasslands that cover 95% of its surface. The surface is highly susceptible to wind erosion if the grassland is disturbed.[139] Below its surface lie hundreds of feet of coarse sand and gravel. Essentially, the porous soil acts like a giant sponge that quickly absorbs precipitation, allowing very little to run off. In some areas, the water table reaches the land surface—a characteristic that creates lakes that dot the region as well as 1.3 million acres of wetlands.

The Sand Hills sits atop the Ogallala Aquifer—one of the largest aquifer systems in the world.[140] The highly porous soil of the Sand Hills make the area a significant recharge zone in the northern region of the Ogallala Aquifer system. That is, the sandy, porous soil of the Sand Hills allows a significant amount of surface water to enter (recharge) the aquifer system. Water from the aquifer also accounts for a significant amount of water use—78% of the region's public water, 83% of irrigation water in Nebraska, and 30% of water used in the U.S. for irrigation and agriculture.

In the final EIS, the preferred pipeline route through Nebraska would have been located entirely above the Ogallala Aquifer. Potential impacts to the Ogallala Aquifer and the Sand Hills identified in the final EIS include potential groundwater contamination after a release (e.g., a spill or leak from a hole or damaged portion of the pipeline) of crude oil during the construction or operation of the proposed pipeline. Both the soil porosity and the close proximity of groundwater

---

[136] U.S. Department of State press release, "Keystone XL Final Environmental Impact Statement Released; Public Meetings Set," August 26, 2011, http://www.state.gov/r/pa/prs/ps/2011/08/171082 htm.

[137] These additional public meetings are not part of the NEPA process. Considering the strong public interest in the pipeline proposal (both opposed and in favor), the public hearings were part of the State Department's national interest determination.

[138] U.S. Department of State, November 10, 2011.

[139] For more information, see the Department of the Interior's U.S. Fish and Wildlife Service web page on the Sand Hills at http://www fws.gov/mountain-prairie/pfw/ne/ne4 htm.

[140] The entire Ogallala Aquifer system stretches across eight states generally from north to south to include South Dakota, Nebraska, Wyoming, Colorado, Kansas, Oklahoma, New Mexico, and Texas and underlies about 174,000 square miles.

to the surface increase the potential that a release of oil from the pipeline could contaminate groundwater in the region.

During the public review period, the Governor of Nebraska called a special session of the legislature to determine if siting legislation could be crafted and passed for pipeline routing in Nebraska. Facing the prospect of new state pipeline siting regulations applicable to the Sand Hills, together with the concern about the Keystone XL pipeline's specific "preferred" route, the State Department announced that it would require additional information about alternative pipeline routes avoiding the environmentally sensitive Sand Hills area in Nebraska before moving forward with its National Interest Determination.[141] Although the State Department did not decide that environmental issues led to a determination that the proposed project was not in the national interest, environmental issues identified in the final EIS, and further stressed in public comments, led to its decision to delay that determination until it gathered this information.

Although no new decision deadline was established, State Department officials suggested that it would be "reasonable to expect that this process including a public comment period on a supplement to the final EIS consistent with NEPA could be completed as early as the first quarter of 2013."[142] In a prior press interview, President Obama also appeared to suggest that, notwithstanding the delegation of Presidential Permit authority to the State Department, he would be personally involved in the final decision on the Keystone XL Pipeline permit application.[143]

Directive to the President to Approve or Deny the Permit

In the wake of the State Department determination that supplemental analysis was needed, Congress directed the President to make a determination on the Presidential permit application for the Keystone XL pipeline. Specifically, the Temporary Payroll Tax Cut Continuation Act of 2011 (P.L. 112-78), enacted on December 23, 2011, included provisions requiring the Secretary of State to issue a permit for the project within 60 days, unless the President publicly determined the project to be not in the national interest.

Subsequently, the State Department, with the President's consent, announced that it would deny the Keystone XL permit on January 18, 2012. In its announcement the department stated that its decision "was predicated on the fact that [P.L. 122-78] ... passed in December does not provide sufficient time to obtain the information that we think is necessary to assess whether the project, in its current state, is in the national interest."[144] However, the department also stated that its decision did not preclude TransCanada from reapplying for a Presidential Permit in the future, although such a reapplication "will trigger ... a completely new review process."[145]

As a result of that denial, instead of developing a supplemental EIS incorporating analysis applicable to a new pipeline route through Nebraska, a new Presidential permit application process will be required. As a result, a "new" NEPA process will be required. Although much of

---

[141] U.S. Department of State, "Keystone XL Pipeline Project Review Process: Decision to Seek Additional Information," Media Note, PRN 2011/1909, Office of the Spokesperson, November 10, 2011.

[142] U.S. Department of State, November 10, 2011.

[143] KETV NewsWatch 7, "Uncut: KETV's Rob McCartney Interviews President Obama," Omaha, NE, November 1, 2011, http://www.ketv.com/video/29652519/detail.html.

[144] U.S. Department of State, January 18, 2012.

[145] Ibid.

---

the analysis and documentation will likely be the same, issuance of a draft and final EIS, and corresponding public and agency comment periods, will be required.

Author Contact Information

Paul W. Parfomak
Specialist in Energy and Infrastructure Policy
pparfomak@crs.loc.gov, 7-0030

Linda Luther
Analyst in Environmental Policy
lluther@crs.loc.gov, 7-6852

Neelesh Nerurkar
Specialist in Energy Policy
nnerurkar@crs.loc.gov, 7-2873

Adam Vann
Legislative Attorney
avann@crs.loc.gov, 7-6978

Acknowledgments

The authors would like to acknowledge the contributions of Kristina Alexander and Vanessa Burrows to the content of this report.

www.ingramcontent.com/pod-product-compliance
Lightning Source LLC
Chambersburg PA
CBHW081405170526
45166CB00010B/3220